The Man Who Was God

*Experiencing the Miracle Worker
in
Today's World*

Margaret Peat

Copyright © Margaret Peat 2022

All rights reserved. No part of this publication may be reproduced, stored in a retrieval system, or transmitted in any form by any means, electronic, mechanical, photocopying or otherwise, without the prior written consent of the publisher. Short extracts may be used for review purposes.

ISBN: 9781914173080

All Scripture quotations are taken from the New International Version unless otherwise stated. Copyright © 1973, 1978 International Bible Society. Published by Hodder and Stoughton.

Editing, design and layout by Life Publications
www.lifepublications.org.uk

Dedication

To Mum and Dad
who told me
the stories of Jesus

Commendations

I love the way Margaret recalls well known Bible stories of the life of Jesus but from the eyes of someone who may or may not have been there. Each chapter reminds us of who Jesus is and how He came to demonstrate the power of God. This book helps us to reflect on our own lives and how we can learn from these stories to grow in faith, wisdom and love.

A great book that not only gives us a new perspective of these accounts but shows us how these lessons can be applied to our daily lives and make us more fruitful. Each story serves a reminder that Jesus came to bring us life, hope and freedom.

Leanne Mallet, Leader of Aspire
National Women's movement in Elim in the UK

Our dear friend, Margaret, who we have known just a few years, has truly inspired us with her books. They are all different, as is every person and there is something in each book to touch every heart.

Margaret's book *The Man Who Was God* is written with a deep insight into people's lives and how Jesus changes them both then and now. It is easy to read, yet challenging, and its chapters can be 'dipped into' for practical everyday situations. A real blessing. Thank you Margaret. May God continue to inspire you by His Holy Spirit.

Keith and Kathy Mashiter
Directors of Centre Light Trust and good friends

As someone who has been a Christian for a long time and who loves the word of God, I was greatly moved when I read Margaret's latest book, *The Man Who Was God*.

She has sensitively and beautifully brought many of Jesus' miracles to life. From turning water into wine, raising people from the dead, casting out demons, healing and speaking to the winds and the waves she has drawn out the cultural issues of the times, and expressed the emotions that those involved would most likely have felt as they came to Jesus for help and received it.

This book is a fitting sequel to The Woman and The Well and the applications Margaret adds to each chapter enable us to explore what a perfect miracle worker Jesus is!

Anne Hinks, youth leader along with her late husband, Stuart, in the 1970s, an inspirational influence in Margaret and Kevin's early life in Derby, England

Ever wondered what it would have been like to be there, to actually see and hear Jesus, to be in His presence when He spoke those words or performed that miracle? *The Man Who Was God* accomplishes exactly that.

This book gives a front row seat on the ministry of Jesus and reveals who He is through the eyes of the people who encountered Him. Reading these chapters, you are pulled into the story and drawn into the life of Jesus and, as you journey through its pages, you find the life of Jesus being formed in you!

This book is packed with powerful storytelling and life changing truth. It is written from a heart that reflects the love of Christ and helps your own heart fall in love with Him too. Margaret writes in a powerful way that truly brings you face to face with *The Man Who Was God!*

After reading just a few chapters I found myself gripped and desperate to see what the next story would be!

Fraser Donaldson
Senior Minister Glasgow Elim Church

If there is one thing that is completely your own, it can never ever be taken from you - it is your story! It is an up-front and personal record of your life; the things you have seen, heard, done, witnessed, lived through and experienced - it is yours!

As I read the Bible each day, I literally try and place myself in the story; try to feel the emotion, the desperation, the anticipation, fear, joy and wonder of what it was like to live then, to have walked and talked or even joked with the disciples or even with Jesus himself. Oh the wonder of it!!

Margaret has literally created that for us in this book. Each chapter may be short but it packs a punch of authenticity & relevance for today that is undeniable. A must-read for those who love the Bible or not … they soon will!

Tom Hatch, Senior Pastor, Elim Christian Centre
Blenheim, New Zealand

Contents

Chapter

1	Saving The Best Until Last	13
2	It Happened At One	17
3	Go Out Into The Deep	23
4	Authority I'd Never Seen Before	27
5	I Could Never Have Done It Without Mother	31
6	He Reached Out And Touched Me	37
7	Just Say The Word	41
8	That's What He Would Like	45
9	Only One	49
10	They're My Pigs	53
11	A Full House	57
12	He Did All He Could	61
13	I Fell At His Feet	67
14	Do You Believe?	71
15	The Light Of My Life	75
16	There's More To See	79
17	And He Stretched Out His Hand	83
18	A Story To Share	87

19	I Couldn't Believe My Eyes	91
20	A Few Extra Crumbs	97
21	Far And Wide	101
22	Up The Mountain	105
23	Tree Spotting	109
24	A Smile On His Face	115
25	The Light Is Here	119
26	The Crowd Cheered	125
27	We Watched The Man Walk Away	129
28	Is There Only You?	133
29	If Only You'd Been Here	139
30	In My Heart I Knew	145
31	Somewhere To Sit	151
32	It Was All A Mistake	155
33	Lost For Words	159
	Other books by Margaret Peat	167

Introduction

Have you ever wanted to sit down and talk with someone who's long gone from this earth? That's how I sometimes feel about the bible. Many of the people in there experienced amazing things and their experiences can often become a blueprint for our life today.

What was it like to actually live when Jesus lived? What was it like to meet him? What was it like to know his involvement with your life? To experience a *miracle*?

What would these people say if they were to sit down with us and tell us what happened?

Hidden between the lines of the bible are millions of actions and reactions, hopes and fears, dreams and disappointments which, right now, we just don't know. So this book is based on some of their own stories from the bible but with added cultural details to illustrate the kind of world in which they lived.

Each miracle is told by someone who may or may not have been there, telling you their story. Some names we know such as Jairus, Malchus and Mary, and others I have created a name to bring their story to life. Here is what might have been as these people met Jesus and their lives were changed forever.

Each chapter has an **application** about some issue that is important to your life. I have put certain phrases in bold letters so you can meditate on these things, chew them over and think them through.

The **prayer** at the end of each chapter is set out in sentences. Feel free to expand each sentence as you are led so you are personalising and applying these prayers to your own life.

And finally, at the end of each chapter is the **bible reference**. Why not take a pencil and your own bible and underline anything in the passage that you'd just never noticed before? It's amazing how we can read a story hundreds of times and there are still things to find.

We all want to live our best life. I pray that as you read about these displays of God's power through Jesus, you too will experience it in your life.

Margaret

1
Saving the Best Until Last
By Adam (devoted servant)

I turned round and there he was. Right behind me. Startled, I stepped backwards and slowly moved to the other side of the room, never taking my eyes off this man about whom I had heard so much.

I had worked for my master for two years, fetching, carrying, caring for his every need but this was the first wedding we were hosting and everything was meticulously planned.

I carried on with my duties, though now continually conscious of where this man Jesus was. Mary, his mother, was there with him and later his friends arrived, those he was teaching and training as he preached his message.

It was when I was passing the six huge stone water jars, late in the afternoon, that I heard Mary question with an urgency in her voice…

"They have no more wine??"

I couldn't believe my ears. We had conscientiously worked out the amount we would need. My blood ran cold as I thought of the consequences of my master being embarrassed in such a way.

Jesus looked at his mother, fully recognising her obvious concern.

"It's nothing to do with me, Mother," I heard Jesus reply as he sat down on the floor.

But Mary could see something in his eyes because before I could remove myself, she suddenly turned and looked at me.

"Adam, do whatever he tells you to do." She obviously trusted him implicitly. Should we do the same or not?

How did I get involved in this? I asked myself as I looked down at Jesus who showed no concern or desire to get involved at that moment. There was an awkward pause and then Jesus spoke.

"Fill the jars with water please," he said.

Each stone jar held twenty to thirty gallons so that was no quick exercise but the master of the house hadn't yet heard the bad news and I was desperate.

As quickly as we could we fetched water and filled each stone jar right up to the brim. Jesus said nothing. He seemed deep in conversation with a small man sitting in the corner across from him.

All six water jars eventually full, I stood for a moment not knowing what to do next. Just as I thought he had forgotten all about the problem, Jesus turned again and looked up.

"Adam, now please draw some out," he instructed, waving his hand at the nearest jar, "and take it to the master of the banquet."

My blood turned even colder as I imagined the master's reaction when I offered him a cup full of cold water! My hands trembled as I scooped up the water from the first jar and then carefully carried it over to where the master was laughing with a group of guests.

It was a moment or two before he noticed me but then he turned and took the cup, bringing it to his lips and taking a long slow drink. He stopped what he was saying, stood for a moment and then peered into the cup. I closed my eyes and waited, my heart beating with fear. He took another drink, this time swilling it round his mouth with a puzzled expression on his face. He was silent.

"Romesh, what is this?" he asked turning to the bridegroom.

"What have you given me to drink?" he asked, turning then to me.

"I, I, I…" I stuttered, unable to bring myself to speak.

"This… this is the best wine I have ever tasted in my life…" he shouted excitedly at the bridegroom.

"Everyone brings the best wine out first and the cheaper wine after everyone has had plenty to drink. You… you have saved the very best until last!"

I couldn't believe what I was hearing. I glanced across the room in relief. There was a somewhat satisfied sort of smile on the face of Mary as I caught her eye at that moment.

Jesus was still in conversation with the small man in the corner.

Trust

To trust sounds an easy thing to do but sometimes it can be very difficult. When things don't happen quite as soon as we have planned, we wonder if they are going to happen at all and it's then **we learn that our Father is never in a hurry.**

Jesus was asking this servant to live on the edge and in that moment when he took what he thought was water to the master, he was certainly doing that. And from time to time our Father asks us also to experience life on the edge. It takes trust.

How amazing that the latter wine was better than the early stuff. How must that have felt when the master declared *"You've saved the best till last?"*

If you feel you've done your bit, you've had your day, the best days are behind you, think again. Or maybe you're in the middle or at the start of your life but you feel that everyone else has all the action. "FOMO" is an identified condition! ***Fear of Missing Out.* Is that you?**

He could just be saving the best till last! Can you trust him to do that?

Remember God is seldom in a hurry.

Prayer

Father, help me to trust you.

When things don't happen as planned and when it seems that events are just the opposite of what I want, help me to trust that you know best and you know what you are doing.

Thank you that you promise that somehow, all things will work together for good.

I trust you Lord.

Amen

Now read John 2:1-11 – *Jesus Turns The Water Into Wine*

2

It Happened at One

By Kuni (servant of a royal official)

I had noticed the boy the previous day. The son of the Royal Official was a precious part of the household and he wasn't his usual lively self and looked pale and listless.

The next day he lay in his bed unable to raise himself and my master was summoned. His nanny and his mother already sat by his side. It was heart breaking to see him lying so still. He was a fun loving, bright, handsome child. He loved life and his presence ensured that everyone around him shared that love too.

I remembered when he had hidden his father's favourite drinking vessel for fun, his eyes shining as he enjoyed the joke. The joke seemed worth the punishment.

I thought of his Bar Mitzvah when he would become thirteen and his future lay ahead of him. The house was always alive with the sound of his voice. Now the house was silent as he lay still on his bed.

The oil lamp was alight and positioned on a stone shelf. It lit up the whole room and shone all night reflecting the sweat on his little face. It was good that there was a separate room from the main living area where he could lie in peace and quiet. In the home in which I grew up, everyone lived and slept in the same room so once someone got up, everyone was awake but, in this house, at least he had some peace.

As the night progressed, he got worse and by the next morning, he looked close to death. His mother, very distraught, refused to leave his side and his father paced the floor, deep anxiety etched across his face as he came and went from his many royal duties.

The next morning his father entered the room dressed, it appeared, for travel. I waited outside as he visited his son, hoping for some improvement in the boy.

But as he left the room, he sadly shook his head as he passed me. Then he stopped and turned, his eyes full of fear.

"The doctor believes there is no hope, Kuni. I have heard Jesus of Nazareth is in Cana again," he said to me. "Remember we heard he turned water into wine? I am going to ask him to come and see my son. He is close to death now and we are desperate. I will do anything to see my son healed."

And then he turned and left the house.

The sixteen miles from Capernaum to Cana would be arduous and difficult in parts. But he was desperate and I knew he would make it. He could be there within seven hours or so.

The day progressed and then the night and there was no change in the boy's condition. At midday, the next day, his mother came from the room and asked me to sit with the child for a while. I quietly settled myself down by his side praying to God Almighty that he would save his life. Peace filled the room and all was still.

It was about one o'clock when there was a movement by my side. I opened my eyes to see the boy looking at me and attempting to sit up.

"Kuni," he whispered. A smile spreading across his face.

"Stay still," I whispered, "You are very sick…"

But he continued to struggle upright. He grabbed my hand and slowly put his feet over the side of the bedroll where he lay. Within a moment he was standing and looking around as though he had just awoken from a deep sleep.

I ran to find his mother, not needing to explain as I was followed closely by her child behind me. His eyes were bright and he was smiling as he ran to her and she took him by his hands hardly able to believe what she was seeing.

"Go and find his father," she said to me. "Take Romesh and Jacob (who were other servants) and tell him he needn't fetch Jesus now." We gathered together our travelling things and set off the sixteen miles to share the wonderful news.

The master was on the way home when we found him.

"The child is living and is well," we shouted as we neared him. "It happened at 1pm."

Our master stopped and smiled. Joy filled his face.

"It was then when I spoke to Jesus," he said. "I told him my child was dying, and begged him to come to the house. He simply turned to me and said 'Your son will live.' Something inside me just believed what he said so I left to come home."

It was when we got home that he gathered his entire household together and told the whole story.

I busied myself by the fire enjoying the amazement of everyone at this miracle, something sent by God to our house.

Pride

I'm sure it wasn't easy for this official to go and ask Jesus for help. A royal official would have had plenty of responsibility, people who looked up to him and an important position. He would have had access to doctors and be well able to manage his office in the royal household and his own household too. He had much to be proud of.

But he was desperate and desperation is one of the things which enables us to move out of the strait jacket of pride. Pride is a deep satisfaction with our own achievements or those of someone else. But it's important not to carry an inflated sense of our own worth, making us feel superior to others. Pride can stop us doing things as **we become over concerned about how they may appear.**

This man was willing to go the journey. The walk was long and hard but he was willing to do it. Sometimes pride stops us from being willing to repair relationships or undertake tasks we feel are beneath us.

It's when we are desperate enough to step out of our prison of pride that we can be amazed at how our Father brings healing into our lives in so many areas.

Prayer

Father God, please show me today those areas in my life that are infiltrated by pride.

I acknowledge today that everything I have and am is by the grace of God. All I have is from you and all I am is by your grace.

Forgive me when I believe that I achieve things by myself or when I see myself as superior to other people.

Thank you Father.

Amen

Now read John 4:43-54 – ***Jesus Heals the Official's Son***

3
Go Out Into The Deep
By Zebedee (father of the Sons of Thunder)

What a night! We had been out the whole of the night and caught nothing.

I sat at the water's edge in the hot sun and closed my eyes for a moment. I could hear the shouts from those of our partner boat as they too sat on the shore washing their nets.

I'm Zebedee by the way and my boys are James and John.

I continued to watch our hired hands wash the nets beside our boat. It was so disappointing after a whole night out on this Lake of Gennesaret.

Suddenly, I heard a voice and looked up to see a man standing not far away. My boys, James and John stopped what they were doing to look at him. There were people starting to crowd around this stranger and after a few minutes he began to speak. I could hear him teaching the Word of God to them.

After a few minutes he looked over at us and walked up to Simon's boat which was at the edge of the lake next to our own. Simon stood up startled and as this man got in his boat, he moved the boat out a little from the shore.

The man continued to teach the people from the boat as they sat on the shore. After he had finished all was quiet for a moment.

"Put out into deep water," I heard him say to Simon, "and let out the nets for a catch."

"We've worked hard all night, both us and Zebedee's boat too and we've caught nothing."

He paused a moment and then continued.

"OK, let's get out there and let down the nets."

I watched as Simon obeyed the instructions and moved his boat out into deeper water and they sat there for a while, the boat bobbing gently on the water.

"Now pull up the net," said this man and as Simon began to do that, I watched with amazement. The net was heavy, loaded with fish. Simon and his brother pulled hard but there were so many fish that the net began to break.

"Get out here and give us a hand!" Andrew shouted to us. James and John jumped into our boat and they were soon out beside them. There were fish everywhere. They began to throw them into our boat and soon it was so full that they began to sink. I watched in amazement.

"Zebedee, look at the fish," someone shouted to me.

"Enough, enough," I called, as I watched from the shore. "You'll be at the bottom of the lake if you take on any more fish!"

I saw that the other boat was just as full and they too were struggling to stay afloat.

Everyone was amazed at the catch of fish they had taken.

"Who is this man?" Simon Peter, waist deep in fish, looked around him as he sat in his boat and he suddenly realised.

"Don't come near me! I am a sinful man!"

Jesus of Nazareth turned to him and spoke.

"Simon, don't be afraid. From now on you will fish not for fish but for people."

The men brought the boats back to shore. Jesus stood and looked around him at Simon and Andrew and at my boys too.

"Follow me," he said to them. Jesus got out of the boat and began to walk away. Our hired men stopped what they were doing and watched. I watched closely too.

Simon and Andrew quickly jumped out of their boat and ran after him. James looked at John for a moment as John gazed after their partners. Jesus turned, looked at them and said,

"Come on, you too…"

Then they gave each other a nod and they too were suddenly on their way running after this man they'd never met, to a future they didn't know.

I walked to the boat with our hired men who were attempting to sort the boatload of fish.

Only one question burned in my mind as I turned and gazed into the distance.

What do I tell their mother?

Obedience

Obedience is the act of yielding to someone's instructions or set of rules. In obeying them, we are submitting to their authority.

It made no sense after a night of fishing to go out and fish again but they followed Jesus' instruction.

I was reading how in the 1800s this word *obedience* was very popular. You may not be surprised to hear that its use has diminished ever since. In these days of the rights of everyone to be heard, to do what they want to do and what feels right for them, obedience is definitely a very unfashionable word.

Why does God ask us to be obedient? Is it purely to chain us to a set of rules which cramp our style and limit our life, or is there something more?

I believe that God knows where the open heavens are going to be in your journey. He wants to bless you in your time on earth and at places along the way, there are points or maybe even a pathway of blessing where he bestows on you a better quality of life, he shares secrets from his heart and pours out an abundance on your life.

How can he direct you to these places? By giving you instructions on earth as to where to position yourself. **There are guidelines written in his word which lead us to those places and as we obey, we position ourselves for blessing.**

The lazy, the proud and the fearful will never find that place of blessing. The obedient will be led to the very place where the heavens are opened.

Prayer

Father, I long to stand under an open heaven.

I long to know your abundance on my life.

Help me, Lord, to hear what you say and do it and to see where you lead and go there. Let my obedience, Lord, be a blessing to you.

Amen

Now read Luke 5:1-11 – *Jesus Calls The Fishermen*

4
Authority I'd Never Seen Before
By Abigail (wife and mother)

This man was amazing. I had never heard teaching like it. His words were so fresh and clear and well, just anointed. He taught with real authority and somehow seemed different from the usual teachers of the synagogue. Even as he stood to teach, even before he spoke, his demeanour carried an authority I had never seen before.

It was the Sabbath day and as was our usual custom, myself, my husband and our family were at the Capernaum Synagogue to worship. We had arrived late and I squashed into the women's area with my two small daughters by my side and my husband and sons sat nearer the front.

For my boys, attending at the synagogue was a daily occurrence as from the age of six they had gone there to learn. Every day, they sat on the ground in a semi-circle facing the teacher with the scriptures as their textbook. Only on a Sabbath did myself and the girls attend there too.

I looked around the synagogue. It was a busy place with services three times a day. This was the centre of social and religious life for many people.

As usual we sang psalms, said prayers, listened to readings from the Scriptures and then settled down for the teaching.

At the front was the ark containing the Scripture scrolls. Nearby, on a raised platform, stood the reader and the prayer leader. One or two stone benches also ran along the walls for some to sit on but I had taken my place with my girls on a mat with the other women towards the back.

A man called Jesus was teaching today and many had crowded in to hear what he had to say. There was much gossip in the town about his ministry as people had witnessed healings he had performed.

All was still, except for the words of this man at the front. Everyone listened with rapt attention. He spoke about real life, about relevant issues. As he spoke, he exuded a sense of confidence, like everything was in control.

Suddenly from out of the silence came a terrifying scream.

"Aaaaaaaaaaaaagh! What do you want Jesus of Nazareth?" I jumped at the sudden noise.

The scribes and the Pharisees seated in front of the platform facing the people sat to attention looking concerned.

I glanced over towards the front where my husband was sitting with our older sons. He would know what to do.

The man continued in an aggressive voice even louder than before.

"Why have you come? Have you come to destroy us? Aaaaaaaaaaaaaaaaaah!" The awful scream echoed round the silent building.

The man was on his feet now.

"I know who you are. The Holy One of God!" The man began to move down the aisle to where my family sat. My sons were on the end of the row and I began to fear for their safety. The man slowly continued down the aisle, all the time shouting at the top of his voice, letting out piercing screams as he moved closer to my children. My heart was now beating fast.

Suddenly, two words cut through the torrent of cries.

"BE QUIET." He spoke with absolute authority.

As he spoke, Jesus looked down to the man who was now standing right beneath him. And then speaking directly to something we couldn't see,

"COME OUT OF HIM."

The people sat in silence as the man suddenly gave a long loud shriek and fell to the floor.

What is this? I thought. *Is it a new teaching? Such authority.* There was no question in my mind that this Jesus was in control.

"Did you see that, Abigail?" said the woman sitting next to me. "He just gave an order and the evil spirit totally obeyed him!"

"I wish my children were as obedient…" she added, as Jesus began to address his congregation once again.

Authority

Wow…what authority. Jesus was continually in touch with his Father above, carefully listening and obeying every prompting.

His authority came from above and, as believers, our Father in heaven has given us authority to use on this earth.

He has a life planned out for you and **he has already given you the tools to thrive, not just to survive.** His plan is for you to thrive.

And yet how many of us use that authority? **Sometimes we are like hungry people with a picnic basket of food which we never stop to open.** Sometimes it's like we are hot and thirsty with a bottle of cool, cold water which we never stop to drink.

We have far more authority than we realize, it's part of our inheritance. On the day we are saved we inherit a place in heaven, gifts to use, fruits of the spirit to share, a family in the church to enjoy and **the name of Jesus to speak over our life.** Jesus secured that authority for you and the power of God will always be there to work on your behalf if you will call on him.

Prayer

Thank you, Father, for opening my eyes to all that you have provided for me to use here on earth.

Help me to realize that one of my most powerful weapons is the name of JESUS.

There is power, healing, forgiveness and authority in that name.

Thank you that you have given me the tools not just to survive but to thrive.

I want to thrive, Lord, and I choose to use the authority you have given me in order that I may do that.

Thank you Father.

Amen

Now read Mark 1:23-27 – *Jesus Casts Out an Evil Spirit*

5
I Could Never Have Done It Without Mother
By Maya (wife of Peter the disciple)

I'd never done this before! In fact, I'd never done a lot of things before that had now become part of my life.

As a fisherman's wife, life was pretty routine really. Looking after the house, making the bread, fetching the water and keeping things running while Peter was away fishing.

Then one day everything changed. It was completely unexpected the day Jesus came into our lives, and without warning, our world was turned upside down and my husband became a fisher of men.

Peter has always been an impetuous man but I've tried to balance that and be there to reason with him, caution him at times and encourage him when times were difficult. But this time was different.

"You do know, Maya, that this man is going to change our lives," Peter had said to me one day. I knew and I was ready.

At least now, on his long trips away from home, I knew my husband was safe on dry land on a stormy night. Before then, many nights had found me awake listening to the wind and rain, praying for the safe arrival of the boat back to land.

He still is absent for long periods. Probably longer actually but I'm already used to that and we're passionate for Jesus and all that he stands for but I'm sure you've already guessed that.

And Jesus was coming to our house for a meal.

We (that's the mother-in-law and I) had tended to every detail in the house, sweeping, polishing and washing everything which could be swept, polished or washed. Ingredients were purchased and prepared. Vegetables, fish, bread, fruit, wine and grains and even meat on this occasion.

I planned that we would cook and eat outside that evening when it was cooler, sitting on the ground around a huge pot, scooping out the tasty dish with pieces of bread and pulling out the meat with our fingers.

I had prepared a bowl of water and a towel to be passed round at the start of the meal for hand washing. I had also placed a bowl by the door and a towel for foot washing on arrival and oil for their heads.

So many things to do and so glad that Peter's mother lived in our home and offered her valuable know how. She was a huge help. In fact, to be truthful, she was the mastermind behind this occasion and we talked and laughed excitedly as we waited for Peter to appear with his brother, Andrew, and also James and John and of course, Jesus.

"Maya, I don't feel too well," she had said. It was in the afternoon that she began to feel unwell. First a headache and then light headedness and eventually, unable to continue her tasks I sent her to bed.

Looking in a while later, I could see that she was in the grip of a fever and incredibly poorly. I hardly dare leave the room. I was seriously worried.

I needed to light the fire and put the pot on it to start cooking but she was so sick that I sat by her side a lot of the afternoon.

It was six o'clock in the evening when the men arrived. By now mother was shaking, her teeth were chattering and sweat ran down her face. The house was silent and not a lot had been done for the meal.

Peter ran into the room where his mother lay.

"What's happening Maya?" he asked quickly. I knew that this visit meant a lot to him.

"Your mother…she's sick" I replied, trying not to sound too distressed.

Peter turned on his heels, left the room and in a moment, Jesus walked into the room.

He looked at her with eyes of compassion. It was clear that he was concerned even though he barely knew her. He walked over to the bed and took her hand. Her eyes opened and she looked into his face.

Amazingly, slowly he began to help her up. She'll never sit up I thought, let alone stand. But as I watched, slowly at first, every movement she made seemed to fill her with strength. She raised her head and her neck was made strong. She sat up and clean air filled her lungs. She swung herself to the side of the bed and her arms were strengthened. Still holding onto Jesus, she slowly stood on her feet and her legs held her firm.

By the time she was on her feet, the fever had left and she was as good as new. Jesus was smiling, obviously enjoying our delight and excitement.

Dinner was a little late that evening but it didn't really matter. We were so excited to have our own real miracle in our midst and so enthralled by the tales and funny stories of the master that time went in a flash.

Mother and I served and then we ate once everyone had had their fill. It was a perfect evening, though I could never have done it without mother!

Help

It was all hands-on-deck that day as Jesus was coming for a meal. Mother-in-law was helping, but no doubt she was the true expertise.

We are all called as Christians, to help others. There are many verses in God's word encouraging us to give assistance to those around us.

It's God's desire that he gives to us and then we pass it on to others. In doing that, we let our light shine and we share God's love on the earth.

When we give to others we give to the Lord and so, when we do it for them, we do it for him.

There is also a principle in the bible called sowing and reaping. What you sow, you will reap, he tells us. **As we pour out our lives in serving others so, too, we will reap blessings in our own life.** He has promised us that when we give to others, he will reward us for doing that.

No one is meant to go through this world by themselves. **Assisting others, sharing blessings you've had, having a conversation with someone and looking out for their needs connects us and brings God's love to them.** As we serve others, we bring his light into the world and let that light within us shine out. As we serve others we will know his presence, we will know his touch and we will know his healing.

Let your light shine.

Prayer

May the love of Jesus shine out of my life, Lord.

Open my eyes to the ways in which I can help others.

I want your light to shine brighter in me in everything I do, for your glory.

Amen

Now read Mark 1:29-31 – ***Jesus Heals Peter's Mother-in-Law***

6
He Reached Out and Touched Me
By Levi (former leper)

It was early one morning that I first noticed the light patches on my skin. I thought nothing of it and continued about my day.

As time went on, I noticed I had decreased sensation on these patches and it was then that I began to worry.

I went straight to the priest for examination and when he said I was infected, I was devastated. I tore my clothes and let my head hang down, shouting to warn people.

"Unclean, unclean."

I was not allowed to come within six feet of another person – including my wife and family – so I moved away from them and lived with other lepers, some who recovered and others who died.

"Levi... Levi..." My wife's cries as I left, resounded in my head night after night.

Muscle weakness came later. Numbness plagued my hands and feet, legs and arms and I knew it was only a matter of time until problems began with my sight. As I looked at the worst cases around me in the leper commune, I could only wonder if their fate would be mine.

The day I went to see Jesus, I had to be so careful. I knew that if anyone recognised me, they would shout at me, push me out of the way or maybe even stone me. When I happened to see him alone with his disciples on the outskirts of the village, I just ran up to him and fell to my knees begging him for his help.

"Jesus, if you want to, I know that you can make me clean again."

I didn't know what he would do but as I knelt before him, he reached out and touched me.

"Levi, I *am* willing," he replied. "Be clean." It was so long since I had felt such kindness that tears filled my eyes.

Immediately I looked down and saw that my leprosy was going. I knew it because I could feel my hands again and the white patches were fading before my eyes. My feet and legs were numb no longer and I felt well.

"I just have to go and share this!"

"Go away and don't say what's happened to anyone," replied Jesus. "Just go and show yourself to the priest and offer a sacrifice."

I set off for the priest but I was so happy, I couldn't believe what had happened. I danced down the street to my family home and as I did, I passed many people on the way. They could see me coming down the road fit and well. Levi, the leper no more!

"Jesus has healed me," I shouted, as I watched them hurry away to find him.

I didn't see Jesus in the town again. He stayed outside the towns in lonely places. Nevertheless, the people still came from everywhere to see him.

I wonder why?

Shame

Shame is a very uncomfortable thing to live with. This painful feeling of humiliation causes us to feel inferior, worthless and isolated from other people

There are many reasons we end up wearing a "shame" coat. Mistakes of the past morally, sexually or relationally can cause years of regret.

But there are other innocent reasons also. Shame about our nationality, gender, marriage or family status and many other things bring us pain which is caused through no fault of our own.

Shame attacks self-esteem as you feel judged by others. Feelings of worthlessness can plague our lives and affect everything we do. We blame others, or ourselves or God for our situation.

Jesus loves to remove "shame" coats. **Whatever you've done or haven't done, whatever you are or aren't, he is not concerned. He longs to remove that shame coat and give you a robe of righteousness in its place.** Whether you feel your shame is deserved or not, he longs that you let it go and live in the freedom of the Father's blessing.

Prayer

Thank you, Father that you are able to lift off my shame.

Sometimes, I feel worthless but I thank you that I do not need to live like this.

Through your death and resurrection, you set me free from shame.

I receive that forgiveness today in Jesus' name.

Amen

Now read Mark 1:40-45 – ***Jesus Heals the Leper***

7

Just Say the Word

By Aelius (Roman centurion)

Judah had been turned into a Province of the Roman Empire a long time ago and now, years later I earned my living from it.

My name is Aelius. As a soldier in the Roman Army I was responsible for one hundred men. My role was to assign duties to those men, maintain discipline, show valour in battle and ensure they stood firm in trials we may face.

I kept good discipline and my men were responsive and obedient, coming and going to my direction. My servants also.

Terah was my favourite servant and on the morning that he didn't appear, I was concerned. He was my longest serving and most reliable servant and it was quite unlike him not to arrive. He was a joy to have around, conscientious, always cheerful, calm under pressure and faithful.

That particular morning, another servant came running with a message.

Terah was paralysed and was unable to leave his bed. He was in pain and suffering terribly.

That day on my way to training legionaries, I passed a crowd surrounding Jesus of Nazareth. He was just finishing his teaching and it so happened that as I passed, he stood up and walked in my direction, the crowd following him. I was in direct line of this man and suddenly a thought crossed my mind.

I took a chance and I went up to him before the crowd surrounded him.

"Lord," I said, "My servant lies at home. He is paralyzed and is suffering badly."

Amazingly Jesus stopped. He looked at me, his eyes piercing deep into my soul.

"Shall I come home with you and heal him?" he asked me. I was quite taken aback. I could not have this man in my house. I did not deserve that but I knew, I just knew as I looked at him that He could heal Terah.

"Just say a word and my servant will be healed. I tell my men to come and go. I say to my servant do this and that. I know that if you speak a word, he will be well."

Jesus seemed to be amazed and turned, saying to his followers, "I've not found anyone in Israel with such great faith."

And then he turned again to me.

"Go. It will happen just as you believe it will."

By the time I arrived home that evening Terah was up and back at his job, more efficient than ever.

Faith

Faith is the currency of heaven.

When we go to a shop, we pay money and receive goods in return. In a similar way, God has given us faith and when we use our faith then we receive in return.

Faith is a bridge we walk along. Sometimes our bridge of faith is rickety and we need to hold on firmly as life tries to tip us off.

But one step after another we slowly make our way towards something that we cannot yet see, but we know is waiting in the heavenlies for us to draw it down to earth.

Sometimes we reach the end of that bridge and God has something different there prepared for us. Then, we have to trust his wisdom in what he provides. Sometimes, it takes more faith to believe when He doesn't provide exactly what we ask for. But we know that all things work together for good, whatever we find at the end of our bridge of faith.

But faith doesn't just come. It's a choice we make. Will you step on that bridge and walk in faith whatever your worries are today?

Prayer

Please help me, Lord, to use the faith you have given me.

Would you increase that faith and strengthen it?

Lord, I make a choice today.

Lord, I choose to believe.

Amen

Now read Matthew 8:5-13 – *Jesus Heals the Centurion's Servant*

8
That's What He Would Like
By Rachel (widow and mother)

We approached the huge town gate, thrown open so the citizens could come and go freely throughout the day. Each day it was shut at nightfall, closed and barred to keep the people of Nain safe throughout the night.

That day as always, the sun was shining, but my emotions were black as night and the gates of my heart had slammed shut that very morning as my only son breathed his last.

A young, strong, fit man, he was a gift of God, working many hours to bring in money to feed us both. When his father died, he became the man of the house and remained that way to this time. His death is a devastating emotional loss to myself and it is a financial calamity to our village.

Young men are precious in Nain, as workers, as protectors, as providers for their wives and fathers to their children and he was the only provider I had. As I had provided everything for him when he was small, he then provided all things for me.

The day had gone in a blur of activity. We watched his final breath and then I closed his eyes, kissed him and we washed his body. As I had washed him as a small child, I now washed him for this final time. I had been there when he came into the world and I was there as he left. I was filled with grief.

Pretty soon, there were many who joined me to anoint him with perfume, nard, myrrh and aloes. We wrapped him in a shroud, covered his face and tied his hands and feet with strips of cloth. And then people came to say goodbye.

I watched with my heart in pieces as relatives and friends picked him up to carry him to his grave. Although my husband had left enough for the anointing, professional mourners were beyond our means and it would be our friends and relatives who would take him on his final journey. That's what he would like, I thought to myself.

The cemetery was over fifty yards outside the village where my son would be placed in the side of a cliff where his father lay. His body would stay there for a year after which we would collect his bones and lovingly lay them at the back of the cave with those of his father and his father's father.

We slowly moved into the street and our noisy procession progressed along the road with the women at the head. They were wailing loudly and throwing dust in their hair but the usual doleful flautists were absent and I was pleased.

As we approached the town gates, there was a crowd moving through from the opposite direction. The men carrying the wooden board on which my son, covered by a shroud, was lying stopped for a moment. The women continued to wail loudly.

Never taking my eyes off him, I waited in the hot sun as the bier began to move off.

"Don't cry…"

The words came out of nowhere then suddenly, he was standing beside me. He was looking at me and I could tell, his heart went out to me. The compassion in this stranger's face was unfathomable to me. I was confused. Who was this man?

The bearers stood still as he went up and touched the bier. And then he spoke once again, not to me but to my son.

"Young man," he said loudly, "I say to you GET UP!"

The women stopped wailing, the crowd stopped talking and it seemed the whole town stood still.

And then my son moved and very slowly lifted his hand. He turned his head, blinked his eyes and gazed in surprise at myself and this man. In that moment of silence there were just three of us in this world. I gazed from one to the other in wonder. And Jesus looked down at us both in compassion, empathy and love.

My son began to sit up and those carrying the bier dropped it in shock and disbelief.

Friends and relatives were filled with awe.

"God has come to his people…" someone shouted as some surged forward to witness this amazing deed.

There were so many people around that I hardly noticed as Jesus took the hand of my son and placed it in my own.

My child looked at me.

"Come, mother," he said to me. "Let's go home."

Compassion

Jesus was a model of compassion. He stood against all that was wrong but his love for those he met was unparalleled.

Action comes from compassion. Compassion is the inward feeling which prompts us to help.

We, too, are called to live showing compassion to those around us and strangers too.

Some people *feel* more compassion than others. That's just how we are wired. But we are all called to *show* compassion.

There was once an experiment carried out where brain activity was recorded as a person showed compassion and helped someone else. It was clear that the outworking of our compassion triggered the brain activity associated with our own pleasure.

Compassion has a good effect on us. When you feel compassion, your heart rate goes down. A smile, or friendly act triggers our body to produce a chemical reaction which motivates us to be even more compassionate. It does the same for those we help as we comfort them.

God made us and we are fearfully and wonderfully made!

Prayer

Lord, let me clearly see what you show me, let me hear what you say but most of all, let me feel what you feel.

Let me live every day with my eyes and ears open and your heart of compassion burning within me.

Lead me today to share your love with my part of your world.

Amen

Now read Luke 7:11-15 – *Jesus Heals the Widow's Son*

9
Only One

By Bartholomew (one of the twelve)

"Move up Bartholomew…" I shuffled along the fishing boat as Jude squashed in beside me.

There we were, all in the boat. Thomas, Simon and Philip were at the front. Simon Peter, Matthew and Andrew down the left-hand side, Judas, James and the other James down the right and John and now Jude either side of me at the back.

Jesus was at the back with us and he and John were laughing at something on the shore. I looked to see but couldn't see what they found so funny.

The fishing boat held about fifteen people. It was a sunny day and the water was calm. We were on the way to the country of the Gadarenes on the eastern shore of the Sea of Galilee.

Often Jesus would teach the people on the shore from the boat but this was a journey with his disciples. As we sailed along, some were snoozing, some talking and some laughing and having a joke. Judas and James moved up to the front to chat with Philip and I talked with Jesus for a while as we sat there in the sunshine.

He was so good to be with. Funny, sincere, understanding but honest and truthful at the same time. I always felt so alive and fulfilled after even a few words with him. I just loved sitting there that day passing the time away on the water.

After a while I saw that Jesus was taking the chance to close his eyes and sleep. He worked hard, public speaking, travelling, healing… it seemed everyone wanted something from him.

The hills around us were fourteen-hundred feet high and the mountains even higher. The mountain slopes dropped sharply down to the sea and it was a breath-taking sight on this hot day. Green hills and deep blue sea, it seemed that we could see any point on the rocky shoreline of the Sea of Galilee. The sea was as smooth as glass and all was quiet.

After a while I noticed a breeze in the air and the four at the front of the boat had stopped talking and were looking ahead. When the wind blew across the eastern mountains and dropped suddenly onto the sea, I knew it could whip up a furious storm in a very short time.

Sure enough, very soon the waves were getting higher and the wind stronger and our fishing boat was tipping this way and that.

Five minutes more, the waves were starting to sweep over the boat and it was slowly collecting water.

We were accustomed to sudden storms on the Sea of Galilee but this severity was quite rare and even the seasoned fishermen amongst us were beginning to look a little concerned.

Everyone was looking around and holding on to whatever they could as they got drenched again and again by the ever-growing waves. The water was cold and took my breath away.

Only one seemed unconcerned. In fact, he wasn't just unconcerned, he was still asleep!

James made his way back down the boat to where Jesus slept.

"Master, we're going to drown in this storm," he shouted above the noise of the howling wind. "Save us…"

Jesus, opening his eyes, looked up at the fearful face above him.

"You have such little faith," he shouted above the noise around us, only just making himself heard above the storm. He looked at me.

"Why are you so afraid, Bartholomew?"

I looked around. Ten-foot waves and wind almost blowing me out of the boat. *Why are we so afraid? Who is this man?* I thought.

Jesus looked around at the disciples in disarray and then, with care, got to his feet.

"BE. QUIET. NOW!" he said loudly. Everyone stopped their cries. We all thought he was talking to us. But those of us near him looked around, hardly believing what we saw. Those at the front of the boat too, noticed the difference and we realised that he had actually addressed the wind and the waves!

Within two minutes, that's all, it was completely calm as Jesus sat once again and closed his eyes.

Jude spoke quietly in my ear.

"Who is this man, that even the winds and waves obey him?"

"No idea Jude," I replied, "but I'm very glad they do…"

Fear

Fear is connected to survival that's why we have a fight or flight response which helps us determine how to stay safe. Fear is an unpleasant emotion we experience when we believe something is dangerous or a threat.

Fears are very real to the person experiencing them. Even irrational fears seem real.

Fear can be inherited or it can be learned and children can become afraid because their parent is afraid. It also comes as a result of experiences as we walk through life.

Scientists tell us that something called Oxytocin (which is released when you are in love) actually helps overcome learned fears. So, when God tells us that his love casts out all fear, that's not just speaking in faith…it's fact!

It's how he created us. When we are filled with God's love, fear can't rule our lives.

Prayer

Please fill me with your love, Lord.

Let your Father's love dissolve my fear.

Fears from the past, fears in the present and fears for the future.

I welcome your Father's love to overwhelm me and fill me today.

Amen

Now read Mark 4:35-41 – *Jesus Calms the Storm*

10

They're My Pigs

By Stepharias (redundant pig keeper)

I'm really glad I don't have to count these pigs, I thought to myself as I looked over our two thousand strong herd of pigs.

My master was Gentile and he had his own reasons for keeping them. My job was just to feed them, shovel their muck and herd them when necessary. It's the most degrading occupation there is but it's a job. Pigs are considered the most unclean animal and to work with them is considered the lowest of the low.

There are not many pig herds in Israel. As you might imagine there's not a great demand for pigs and it's difficult to raise them as they need more moisture than cows or sheep. Nevertheless, there are a few in Gentile families.

When I finished my tasks, I sat for a while looking up towards the tombs where our ancestors are buried. It was quiet up there. That is except for the couple of wild men who lived there roaming about amongst the tombs.

I heard roars at night and sometimes screams which was a bit unnerving but I knew it was them. Everyone said they were mad and I kept well away from them.

It was after I'd just fed the animals. I heard screaming and swearing, which wasn't unusual, and I looked up the hill where I saw a small group of people walking towards the tombs.

I started to run towards them to warn them not to go up there. The two men were very violent, so much so that no one ever passed that way. They would attack anyone who tried to go near them.

Before I could get to them, I saw the two mad men begin to move towards the group. My heart was in my mouth as I continued to hurry towards them. I heard the two men start to shout.

"What do you want with us? Son of God have you come here to torture us?" I stopped in my tracks. The group said nothing or so it seemed.

The men shouted again. "If you drive us out, send us into the herd of pigs."

Hey, they're my pigs I thought, but before I could say anything the leader spoke up.

"Go!" he shouted in a very loud voice.

To my horror I watched as the whole pig herd left their food and suddenly rushed down the steep bank into the lake. All two thousand of them. I couldn't believe what I saw. They were drowning themselves in the water!

I, and those workers with me were terrified and we ran off into the town to tell the master about this great loss and damage. Also, about the two men.

When we went back up into the tombs, the two men looked normal but the townspeople who followed us were not convinced. They were really upset as they looked from one to the other. They pleaded with Jesus to leave.

For me, I just had one burning question. What was I to do with two thousand helpings of pig food?

Surprise

It would certainly be a surprise as those pigs hurtled down the steep bank into the water.

Surprises come in all shapes and sizes and as we negotiate life, we experience situations which we expect, and surprises too.

It is good to know that God knows and plans our future and our life is in his hands. Whatever happens unexpectedly is already in his control.

As we pass through various emotions in our attempt to shift our perspective, he is with us all the way.

It's good to know, as the old song says, that *with God things don't just happen, everything by him is planned*. We can indeed trust him totally as we walk in his pathway for our lives.

Prayer

Thank you, Lord, that you know and plan my future.

Thank you that my life is in your hands.

Thank you that with you, things don't just happen and whatever comes my way – you are in control.

Amen

Now read Matthew 8:28-34 – ***Jesus Sets Two Men Free***

11

A Full House

By Leah (awestruck wife and mother)

My house had never been so full. There were people everywhere.

It was really no more than a large room with a smaller back room for the animals to sleep at night but it was big enough for myself, my husband, his parents and our three children.

Never before had there been this many people in the house. There were people sitting on the low table where we reclined to eat each day and more on the two chests where we stored most of our belongings.

People even started filling the back room where the animals slept and when that was full, I saw them going up onto the roof. The roof had a slight slope, just enough to drain off the rainwater which we would carefully collect into large containers. Every drop of water was precious to us.

Our roof was really an open second floor and had a guard rail around the edge to make it safe. I would store things up there, put out washing to dry and we would sometimes sit and talk there in the evening. Sometimes we'd even sleep up there too.

Actually, the roof was ready for its annual repair. The wooden trusses always held firm but the straw mats which were covered over with hard clay needed annual repairs. We used to do that just before the rainy season and it was ready. In parts I could actually see through it.

Everyone settled down and the people went quiet.

I felt proud that Jesus had chosen our house to visit. I saw my husband standing at the door, who motioned to me with his eyes towards the teachers of the law who sat there too. No doubt they would be checking what was being said in our home. I could see many people behind him in the doorway waiting outside, hoping to hear a word from this man called Jesus.

Just as Jesus was about to begin, there was a noise. It came from above. For a horrible moment I thought the roof was about to give way but then I realised that someone was pulling at the straw mats and clay. I was a little annoyed that they would vandalise our property just so they could hear better but Jesus waited and watched what was unfolding before him. So did everyone else.

The hole just kept getting bigger and bigger and bits of clay and matting was falling on the people below. Whoever was above was determined to get in.

We continued to watch as a stretcher appeared above us along with someone on it and slowly and very carefully it was being lowered down through the hole in the roof. People below pressed together to make room for this to settle on the floor, along with the paralysed man thereon.

Once I saw him and how he was completely unable to move I forgot about my roof and felt my heart reach out to him.

Jesus looked down at him in amusement and then laughed as he looked up at the four faces who peered through the hole.

"Your sins are forgiven," he said to the man, looking down again. He regarded him thoughtfully for a moment and then he looked up, across the room.

"I want you to know," he said pointing across to the teachers of the law, "that I have authority on earth to forgive sins."

I knew they would have been horrified as they heard those words. In their minds, only God could forgive sins.

They just glared at him and said nothing.

Then Jesus looked down and as compassionately as I have ever heard, said to the poor man, "Get up now. Take your mat. Go home."

And as we watched, the man did just that. He carefully got to his feet, picked up his mat and left the room. The crowd around him cheered as they saw it happen before their very eyes.

I kept looking at the roof during the next hour of Jesus' talk. Should we mend it before the rainy season or should we keep it to remind us of what happened today? No, Jacob would never agree to that. But at least I could keep it till he got round to mending it. Who knows? It could be a while!

Determination

They say that determination is more important to success than ability. The bible is quite clear that we are to continue pressing forward in the Christian walk no matter what the circumstances.

Determination can transform your progress and keep you moving forward when times get hard. **If you fail, determination sets you back on the path and failure becomes simply a pause, not an end.** God urges us to see the goal clearly, to set our eyes on that and to keep our eyes on it.

As we believe God to create paths for us to walk towards that goal, our faith in him and in the ability he gives us to do that, continue to take us forward.

Determination can help us in completing our Christian walk to the end, but also in those things we feel called to achieve during that walk.

As we move towards the goals God directs us to, let's also be grateful for the progress we have made and the blessings we have received. **Allow gratefulness to become a wind behind you to spur you on to greater progress in your journey with him.**

Prayer

You, Lord, determined my ability, but my determination belongs to me.

Lord, I want to serve you with all my heart and today I say that I am determined to achieve all you call me to.

You have given me so much, Lord.

Let my gratefulness spur me on to greater things day by day.

Amen

Now read Matthew 9:1-8 – *Jesus Heals the Paralysed Man*

12

He Did All He Could

By Jairus (synagogue leader)

It had been a busy day. As Synagogue Leader there was always much to do. I was the official appointed by the elders to look after the building, to keep its contents safe and to make arrangements for the worship there.

My executive officer handled the details of the synagogue service. Lay people read the prayers and scripture readings and visiting preachers came too.

The synagogue is the centre of community and religious life for us all so it's a place of community, of celebration and of friendship.

The building was not only used as a community centre but also a school, a meeting place, a place of prayer and sometimes even a court room. Many Jews visited the temple at Passover, at Shavuot, Pesach and at Sukkot but the rest of the time they worshipped in the synagogue.

That day had consisted of liaising with my assistant regarding the details of the week and my involvement in the three services that we held each day. Although the lay people were involved, we ourselves planned the rota for each service, we decided who would read and what they would read and I spent some time on future rotas also.

Later, I took a look in the school where the boys were learning and then went home.

It was unusual that my twelve-year-old daughter wasn't looking out for my arrival but she was nowhere to be seen. I entered the house to an incredibly worried looking wife.

"Jairus…Miriam is ill," she said, her face etched with concern. "The doctor has been called for and will be here anytime."

I went to see her and she indeed looked very ill. When the doctor arrived, he spent a long time in the room. Eventually he came out and closed the door. I could see by his face something was terribly wrong. He looked at me and shook his head and I knew the worst had happened.

"I am so sorry, Jairus," he said and then he left.

My wife and I went in to our dead child and sat with her a while. My wife was inconsolable. To me it felt like our world had ended.

Servants spread the news and people started arriving at the house. Someone arranged for the flautists who began their melancholy music. Inside the house it was noisy. From our daughter's room we could hear the noise through the stone wall but still we sat there.

I could not bear to stay for the preparation of her body so I walked round the town not knowing where to go. I felt in despair.

And then I saw Jesus. He was just sitting there in front of me. Immediately I went and knelt before him. I was nobody and this man was healing hundreds. Would he help me?

"Sir, my daughter has died. But if you will come and lay hands on her, I know that she will live again." The tears coursed down my face.

Jesus got up and so I led the way to our home. Jesus and all his disciples.

When he entered our house, the noise was deafening, there were crowds of people in there by that time many wailing and crying loudly. The flautists were playing music and it was a chaotic scene.

Jesus raised his arms.

"Go away," he said to the crowd. "Get out. The girl is not dead. The girl is just sleeping."

The people looked at him in amazement and some started to laugh. But Jesus insisted that they go outside.

Once the house was quiet, he went to her and stood by her side. My wife and I waited at the door.

He said nothing but looked intently at her lifeless body and then lifted his hand and took her hand in his.

"Arise..."

The moment he touched her it seemed that life flowed back into her. She opened her eyes, looked around and then she sat up. Seeing us in the room, she jumped up and ran to us flinging her arms round us both.

"Give her something to eat, she will be hungry," Jesus said.

It was as though she had been on a long journey and was returning home.

We were filled with immense gratitude and after we had offered our eternal thanks to him, we three stood at the door as he left, followed by the many people who had filled our house.

Humility

It would have been easy for the synagogue leader to feel he was too important to go and ask Jesus for help. But instead, he showed humility as he knelt before the Master in trust. The Christian faith is often ironic and surprising, sometimes asking from us exactly the opposite of what we would expect it to. We are clearly told that if we want to be first, we must be last, turn the other cheek and put others before ourselves.

Apparently humble people handle stress more effectively and experience better physical and mental wellbeing. As they show greater generosity, helpfulness and gratitude they create a welcoming environment around them for others to draw close to.

Sometimes humility can be mistaken for a sign of weakness when in fact it's a sign of great inner strength.

When I am with a humble person, **I know that I'm being accepted for who I am, without judgement, and this allows my protective walls to come down.**

As we too, ground ourselves in what God thinks of us **and we value what we are, instead of what we aren't then this cultivates a tremendous inner strength.**

As we begin to understand that sometimes we fail but even so, we are unconditionally loved by our Father in heaven, as we allow him to fill that loveless space and as we make gratitude a more powerful part of our lives then we can walk on with integrity and humility in his strength.

Prayer

Help me to walk in humility, Lord.

Help me to create a welcoming environment around me for others to draw close to, by my generosity, helpfulness and gratitude.

As you showed humility on this earth, help me to live likewise and draw others to you.

Amen

Now read Mark 5:21-24, 35-43 – ***Jesus Heals Jairus' Daughter***

13

I Fell At His Feet

By Naomi (former invalid)

Twelve years had been an eternity! I had been bleeding for twelve whole years. It started one day and never stopped.

I had been used to being unclean for seven days, once a month, confined to social and religious isolation like all the other women, but then my unclean week became longer until it became continual and this had been non-stop for years.

There was little access to medical care for me but I had some money and saw several doctors. The care of those doctors had failed to heal me – in fact things had just got worse.

Many of our doctors seem to prefer to talk about illnesses rather than treat them and in any case, I had spent all I had trying to find a cure. I was disappointed, poor and lonely, separated for many years from all contact with the outside world.

Life expectancy was short. Children were often not adults before their parents were dead. Sixty per cent of one-year-olds were dead by the time they were sixteen years old and a person in a lower class had a life expectancy of just twenty years old.

Poor housing, no sanitation, inaccessible medical care and bad diet kept that life expectancy forever low.

But I was blessed. I had made it to adulthood. But then my misery began.

I'd heard about this man Jesus but I was afraid to go out where the people were. It was one morning on the spur of the moment that I made the decision and I left the house and headed off in the direction of the sound of the crowd. There were people everywhere and I stood and watched for a short time before I carefully pushed my way through the melee to the centre of the crowd.

Jesus was speaking to a man, as I came up behind him I stood for a moment not knowing what to do. It was very noisy and there were so many people demanding his attention. Suddenly, I was filled with faith. *If I can only touch him, I know I will be made well*, I thought. Immediately I was filled with courage. I had to act now!

So there and then I bent down and touched the hem of his garment. As soon as I made contact with it, I felt heat run through my body; right down my arm then all over me. In that moment, I knew I had been healed. I immediately let go of his garment and then I turned to leave before anyone recognised me.

But before I could move, Jesus stopped what he was saying.

"Who touched me?" I heard him ask. I held my breath.

"Master, everyone is touching you, there are many."

"I know power has gone out from me," he replied. I was mortified. My heart was beating so hard I could almost hear it. I fell at his feet with waves of his power still flowing through me.

"Forgive me, Master," I heard myself cry.

"Your faith has healed you." He spoke in a reassuring voice. "Go in peace."

One touch, I thought later that night as I planned all the places I would go and people I would see.

The new life of Naomi was about to begin!

Courage

People who live courageously are said to have fewer regrets in life. They appear to be more successful as their courageous attitude brings more influence and creates stronger ties with those around them. You see life from a better perspective with courage.

But how do you acquire courage? The bible encourages us to be bold and be strong as we negotiate life – but how do we do that? **It's good to know that courage isn't inherited, it's developed.** As we step out believing that God is for us, our courage grows and grows.

Courage inspires you to fulfil your dreams, it helps you attempt new ideas and it allows you to speak up when you would prefer not to. People are not courageous because they want to be. **They show courage because they believe that the result is worth the journey to get there.**

For Christians, courage is available from God. As you come to him with your challenges, he will fill you with a boldness and courage you have never known before.

Prayer

Lord, help me to be bold and be strong knowing that you are by my side.

Even now let the boldness of God grow within me.

Let that courage be evident more and more, as I learn to trust in you in greater and greater measure.

Amen

Now read Matthew 9:20-22 – *Jesus Heals the Woman With the Issue of Blood*

14

Do You Believe?

By Japhet (former blind man)

"Get away you blind beggar!"

I heard him but as always, I couldn't see him. The insults were common but the occasional physical assaults were even worse.

That's why Josiah and I had started to sit together each day.

I bumped into him one day, physically I mean, and we realised that neither of us could see. We became a support for one another.

"Japhet, most people think that it's some huge sin we've committed that's caused our blindness," Josiah said to me one day. We had talked about this a lot. I just didn't know.

I couldn't earn a living so I spent my time on the streets begging for what little I was given.

There were actually laws to help the blind, such as prohibiting the giving of misleading directions to the blind or doing anything to cause us to stumble. Some people followed these laws but some people didn't and many blind were mistreated.

There were various medical treatments for those with money. Some doctors used salves to help and some tried lancing boils or removing inverted eyelashes! Most treatments didn't work.

Josiah and I often spent time in the marketplace where there were others similar to us. Piram was born blind and for Samuel, blindness came after an infection. Some had survived leprosy and some were just aged.

But myself and my companions had two things in common. We were all blind and we all wanted to see.

That's why when Josiah heard that the man called Jesus was in town my heart leapt as I'd heard gossip about the many blind people he had healed.

We quickly followed the noise of the crowd and then some kind man helped us make our way to where Jesus was standing.

"Oh dear," said the man suddenly with disappointment, "he's gone into a house!"

"Quick, take us in," we said in unison.

And so we found ourselves inside a house, hearing the voice of Jesus as he began to teach.

After a few minutes he stopped. And then I could hear him right in front of us. He waited a moment before he spoke.

"Do you believe that I can actually heal you?" he asked.

"Yes Lord," we replied, again in unison.

Then I felt hands touch my eyes.

"According to your faith, it is done," he proclaimed with authority.

I stood for a moment blinking in the increasing brightness. Suddenly, I could see. I COULD SEE! I looked at Josiah. I'd never seen him before but here was my friend looking round too with a huge grin on his thin wrinkled face.

We turned to go but Jesus spoke again.

"Do not tell anyone about this," he replied firmly as we stood in the doorway marvelling at all we saw outside.

"Trees!" I shouted out.

"Houses!" replied my friend.

"Mountains..."

"People..."

And that's how we ran down the pathway. We were bursting. It really was joy unspeakable!

And pretty soon those that we passed realised that we could actually see the things we were shouting out.

I couldn't keep it in. It just kept coming out.

"I want to tell the world..." I shouted, "...that I'm off to see the sunset..."

Joy

The two men must have been bursting with happiness and joy as they left Jesus that day.

In life, occasions, people and possessions can bring us much happiness. But as believers, we are promised joy whatever situation we find ourselves in because joy is different from happiness.

When we experience satisfaction, contentment and great pleasure because of a circumstance or experience **these things often make us happy in the moment but it rarely lasts.**

Joy is a fruit of the Spirit and when we are filled with His Holy Spirit, we experience joy whatever our circumstances. We can obtain happiness when we do something pleasurable but **we know joy when we experience the presence of God filling our lives and overflowing into our emotions.**

I guess the two men above were incredibly happy with their miracle, but they would also have known real joy, being touched by the Master.

Prayer

Thank you Lord, for those things which daily bring me happiness.

For my friends, family, the food you provide and the many little blessings you shower upon me.

But I thank you too for that joy deep down that does not depend on circumstances.

Let that joy bubble up afresh today, right now.

Amen

Now read Matthew 9:27-31 – *The Two Blind Men*

15
The Light of My Life
By Shem (very proud father)

I gazed at the oil lamp which was standing on a stone shelf coming out from the wall. It lit the entire room casting dancing shadows around the room as it flickered.

It would shine all night long and would only be blown out when morning light came. Generally, every home had a lamp lit in their house at night. Only very poor people would not light a lamp.

We had already laid out the bedrolls on the floor. We slept in a row, myself and my wife at either end and the children in between us. I smiled as I looked at my little ones already fast asleep. They were the light of my life.

"Benjamin came home from the synagogue upset today, Shem," my wife had said earlier that evening. "Someone called him names and made fun of him saying his father was a dumb beggar…shouting after him as he came home."

I may be dumb but I wasn't a beggar and never intended to be. But it still hurt me to think that my son was bearing the pain for my infirmity. I couldn't speak to comfort him but as I'd sat him on my knee before bed, I'd given him an extra hug to let him know that I understood his pain. I'd been called many names as a child and had much pain as a result of being dumb. As I sat there, my heart ached.

I wanted to say so much: that it doesn't matter what others say, that what matters is how you live your life. It doesn't matter what others think as long as you know in your heart that you please God and you live a life to benefit other people. But I couldn't say the words I longed to say and I could comfort him only with my arms around him.

I lay on my bed that night and thought a lot, and as I tossed and turned, I made a decision.

I got up early and we packed away the bedroll and ate the bread, grapes and cheese for breakfast, set out by my wife on the floor.

Very soon I was ready to go and I made my way to find Jesus of Nazareth. I had heard such amazing things about him and I was desperate for someone to help me.

I went to stand with a group of strangers and when they spoke to me, I pointed to my mouth to indicate that I could not reply.

Immediately they grabbed my arm and led me towards Jesus.

"He can't speak," they told him, gesturing towards me.

Jesus looked at me for a moment and then spoke with authority.

"Demon come out of him," he said looking right through me.

Suddenly I felt something come up and out of me like a strong wind.

"What was that?" I exclaimed in shock. Everyone looked at me aghast. I realised I had spoken!

I had spoken!!!

The crowd were amazed. "We've never seen anything like this in Israel," they were saying to each other.

This grace of God to me was so amazing. I couldn't wait to get home. I had so much to say to my son.

Grace

What a great ending to the day for that man. He certainly felt God's grace that day.

When I first became a Christian, I learned that *God's grace is unmerited favour, blessings we don't necessarily deserve but which God showers down simply because he wants us to have them.* In other words, you can't earn them, they are free!

We can't earn God's grace, but we can attract it. So how do we attract God's grace and favour?

When we align our lives with what God wants, when we love the things God loves and separate ourselves from those things God hates then we attract God's increased provision and grace into our lives.

But it's not for us alone. As we share his blessings with others God sees we have room for more and we become a conduit, **a channel for distributing blessings** to all around us.

Prayer

Father, I thank you that every day I know your grace.

So many blessings you shower down on my life.

Lord, I want to pay that grace forward into the lives of those around me.

Lead me to those you have already chosen to receive your grace through me.

Amen

Now read Matthew 9:32-34 – ***The Dumb Man***

16

There's More to See
By Onan (former invalid)

I sat in the porch on my mat and my eyes scanned the walls. And then the ceiling. And then the floor. I knew every inch of this place.

I didn't always sit in this porch. There were five of them but I knew every one of them in detail. They gave shelter to the hundreds of sick people who came and sat there, day after day.

Each porch looks out onto the pool of Bethesda and there's always plenty going on at the pool.

My eyes rested on the Sheep Gate through which, on a week day, many hundreds of people streamed in. Some faces I knew well but many I'd never seen before.

I imagined the sheep, having been gathered from the countryside being brought into the temple for sacrifice. Everyone knows, no lamb ever comes back out once it's passed through the Sheep Gate into the temple.

The voices of the people always echoed off the water and rebounded across the porches and there was a constant bustle through the gate.

Today it was quiet though as it was the Sabbath. Most families were at rest in their homes but we were there as usual.

We sat by that pool of Bethesda day after day, lame, paralysed, blind and dumb. The purpose of the pool is to collect rainwater for temple use but there's a second use too and that's why I was there. We were waiting for the still, cool waters of the pool to be stirred.

For thirty-eight long years, I had been sitting by this pool day after day. Some may say it was patience, others said I was a fool. Time after time, I watched as others were the first to enter the pool each time the waters stirred, for a chance of being healed. I sometimes wondered why I went at all, as I had no chance or hope of being the first. But still I went. I had nowhere else to go.

I closed my eyes to the heat of the day and suddenly I heard a voice above me.

"Onan, do you want to get well?" I looked up at the man in front of me. He was speaking to me.

I replied uncertainly.

"I have no one to assist me to get into the pool when the water is stirred…" *Who was this man?*

The man hesitated a moment and then spoke again firmly but with kindness.

"Get up," he commanded. "Pick up your mat."

He paused again.

"Walk."

The whole porch went silent as all eyes were fixed on me and the man who stood by my side.

I hesitated. Everyone knew I couldn't walk. Everyone knew I couldn't even stand. The friends that brought me would come back at some point and take me home. But it was the middle of the day and they were nowhere to be seen. I felt confused and more than a little fearful but there was something in the eyes of this man that meant what he said.

So very slowly and carefully, I began to stand. Hesitantly at first but the more I moved, the stronger I felt and before long I was standing looking into the face of this stranger before me.

Everyone was aghast but in just a moment, the waters had moved and there was a flurry of activity as people rushed to enter the waters and I was forgotten.

The man walked on and I was left alone. Had this really happened? Of course it had. I was on my feet wasn't I? I bent, picked up my mat and went to find my friends.

Patience

If you're forty-five years old or over, try to think back thirty-eight years. What were you doing? Where did you live? It's a long time!

It's hard to imagine the man going to the same place for thirty-eight whole years. That's nearly fourteen thousand days. And he still went!

If there's one thing that we don't like, it's having to wait. In an instant world where everything happens immediately it gets harder and harder to wait around for something to happen.

Patience is a virtue my mother used to say to me. It certainly makes life more comfortable.

Sometimes waiting involves going through uncomfortable circumstances. **Waiting creates space in your life for you to**

step back and assess what's important to you. During this time, you develop persistence, determination and flexibility.

We learn patience by practising it. It is an exercise in self-control as we stop ourselves becoming upset when we feel things are not moving on as fast as we wish.

When we are impatient we make foolish decisions and patience ensures we make the right ones. Patience helps us focus on our goal and increases our desire to reach it. It gives us time to develop skills, it improves our health as we avoid the stress impatience brings. **As we find peace in our place of waiting, it can only improve our life.**

Prayer

Please Lord, fill me with your Holy Spirit and let the fruits of your Spirit become more evident in my life day by day.

Let the fruit of patience grow strong and healthy and flourish in my life.

Please help me to use the time of waiting, to prepare in faith for your perfect time.

Amen

Now read John 5:1-15 – *The Invalid at the Pool*

17
And He Stretched Out His Hand
By David (amazed Pharisee)

It just had to stop. This person was a liability to our land. More and more people were following this man called Jesus.

"We must find a reason to bring charges against him," said Joseph in exasperation. "We cannot let this continue any longer…"

I, myself had not seen this Jesus but I'd heard plenty about him. Often, my wife shared the gossip from her visits to the well and it was clear that he had a loyal following.

Apparently, there were some men who were with him all the time and many others who also went along to hear the stories he told and see the things he did.

We continued our meeting discussing back and forth how to deal with this problem.

"He doesn't follow the law, David," someone said to me.

"He doesn't fast on Mondays and Thursdays," said another.

"He doesn't keep the Sabbath."

Opinions came thick and fast. It was the general thought that he seemed to go out of his way to cut across all that we stood for.

It was the Sabbath when Joanna and I saw him for the first time. He was surrounded by a small group of people and was moving through the group touching some of them and smiling at many of them. I could see that the people were delighted.

"You really do need to pray for wisdom," said Joanna as we moved closer to see what was happening and Jesus laid his hands over a woman's ears.

Yet again this man was disobeying the laws of our religion. It was the Sabbath day which was set apart for rest and prayer.

I had to speak up. I couldn't help myself.

"Is it lawful to heal on the Sabbath?" I shouted across to him.

He stopped and turned and looked at me with interest.

"If you, if any of you," he said looking around, "have a sheep and it accidentally fell down into a pit and it was the Sabbath day, would you go and lift it out or would you leave it?"

No one spoke.

He looked back at myself.

"How much more a person matters to God than a sheep. Therefore, before God it is right to do good on the Sabbath."

And with that he turned and looked around and his eyes rested on a man a little way away.

He was a young, strong man, but his right hand was thin and small and wrinkled. It looked like the hand of a very old man.

I knew by just looking at him that the most valuable part of him, his dominant hand, was useless. His right hand couldn't work or earn him money. He was poorly dressed; I would imagine in great poverty but he had come to the synagogue with his friends and neighbours on this Sabbath day.

"Stretch out your hand," Jesus instructed the man.

The man regarded him, surprised at being addressed by Jesus.

Jesus waited.

And then he stretched out his hand towards him and as he did, we saw it.

We saw the miracle take place. My wife gasped by my side as we watched the hand change. The bones grew and filled the skin and the wrinkles disappeared. We visibly saw the old, withered hand grow strong and young.

I blinked as I watched it for myself.

The stunned man lifted both his hands and looked at them, front and back. They were exactly the same. The crowd were bewildered.

The man began to thank this stranger but Jesus was already walking away.

I looked at my wife. She looked up at me. And neither of us said a word.

Wisdom

Everyone is looking for wisdom.

The officials in Jesus' day were looking for wisdom. They were wanting to make the right decision but they did not have the eyes to see that Jesus was the one the Jews had been waiting for, so they were making all the wrong decisions. They were searching for conventional wisdom when God was doing a brand-new thing which they did not recognise.

It's sometimes hard to make the right decision. The world now advises, *if it feels right and it hurts no one else, do it...* and we can clearly see the direction this leads.

Apparently, **early adversity in life seems to be a factor in the growth of wisdom.** Wisdom comes if we learn from our experiences.

Wisdom is not always recognised. Socrates, Confucius, Martin Luther King etc were wise men but all marginalised or persecuted and when we make wise decisions sometimes, they are not the most popular resolutions.

The book of Proverbs speaks a lot about wisdom which is **one of the most precious things we can have. Our whole life is affected by the amount of wisdom we have** and unwise decisions can have lifelong consequences.

God will lead us on with his wisdom as we follow his Word.

Prayer

Father God, wisdom is one of the most valuable gifts I can have.

In this day where often, right seems to be wrong and where wrong seems to be right, would you please give me your wisdom.

Let that wisdom be the baseline on which I build my life.

Amen

Now read Matthew 12:10-13 – *The Man with the Withered Hand*

18

A Story to Share

By Abigail (very grateful mother)

I was old then and it seemed that, which I had spent much of my life praying for, would never come to pass. My son, possessed with a spirit that had kept him blind and mute, had a very heavy load to bear.

I am Abigail and a widow; he was my only child and I cannot describe the fear that gripped my heart when I thought of leaving him alone on this earth.

He was my life and I was his. He went where I went and most of the time people welcomed him as they welcomed me because he belonged to me. To our people, visitors are sent by God even if they are blind and mute.

It was two days after the Sabbath when I met Rhoda.

"Rejoice Abigail," she greeted me.

"Greetings Rhoda," I replied.

She invited us back to her home nearby and as we entered, her sister grasped my shoulders, drew me near and kissed me on the right cheek and then on the left.

Simeon stood obediently by my side as I removed my sandals and then guided him to a place on the floor. We sat cross legged on the rug. My legs hurt nowadays but a lifetime of crossing my legs ensured I could still follow the custom.

We ate with our fingers, dipping bread into the thick stew carefully set down in the middle of the rug.

It was while we were eating that Rhoda told me something that would change my life.

"Jesus of Nazareth is in town, Abigail, and after the meal we are going to find him."

No amount of reticence on my part changed her mind and it seemed only a moment before we were standing by his side. My son and I.

He looked down at us with compassion

"He's blind and mute," I told him. "He has a demon which prevents him speaking or seeing."

"I know," he replied and he lifted his hand and held it up over Simeon.

I stood watching. Simeon was still for a few moments and then…

"Mother, I can see!" he exclaimed starting to look round in wonder.

"You can talk as well!" I screamed in excitement.

"You have eyes to see, a voice to speak and you certainly have a story to share."

Peace

Imagine the turmoil in these lives. Imagine the fear in this mother's life as she envisaged leaving her only son on this earth alone. Imagine the storm inside as she thought about his remaining days on earth without her.

So, too, in our own lives we have worries and from time to time we have real storms which rage within our minds.

One of the really special things God has promised us is *a peace which passes understanding*. That means it doesn't make sense. When all around seems to be broken, destroyed or flying around our ears God has given us a peace to draw on. **It is already within us. It is already given to us.**

God's peace is so much more than serenity, coolness or stillness. It is something which would seem impossible when we are surrounded by storms but **it comes from within and its source is the Holy Spirit who already lives within us.**

A fruit of the Holy Spirit is peace. As we become still in his presence, fix our eyes on him, allowing all around to grow dim and we thank Him that His peace fills us then we can experience this thing which doesn't make sense.

We too have eyes to see Him, a voice to thank Him and as a result will have a story to share.

Prayer

Thank you Lord, for the peace you give which passes understanding.

Thank you that even in the midst of life altering circumstances, I can know a peace within me and around me which comes from God alone.

I open my heart afresh to that peace. Please let it well up within me right now.

Amen

Now read Matthew 12:22 – ***The Blind and Dumb Man***

19
I Couldn't Believe My Eyes
By Adam (junior disciple)

I watched my mother pour the flour into the bowl and mix it with water.

"Don't eat it all at once." Looking down at me she kneaded it in the small wooden bowl as she spoke.

"And remember once it gets dark, Adam, it's hard to find the way home so don't stay too long."

She added the leaven and then set it to stand for a while.

As always, it was barley bread. Only those with more money had wheat bread but I was thankful for what I got.

"And don't share it round or you'll go hungry," she added. There was no risk of that, I thought.

"No mother," I replied as I stood on my tiptoes to see into the bowl.

She let the mixture stand for a while and then the dough was divided into round, flat cakes. Finally, she put the bread into a stone jar about three feet high which was heated up inside with burning wood. That was our household oven.

A while later I was ready to go, carrying my five small loaves plus two small fish, cooked and packed ready for my trip.

Then one last word.

"Adam, be good," she called as I left the house.

I was so excited.

I had never seen Jesus before and as I made my way to where he was teaching that day, there were many people travelling too. My aunt and uncle were nearby and I kept a close eye on them.

We walked for a long way and once there, I soon found myself a little spot in the middle of a field and settled down ready to listen to what he had to say. I looked around while I waited and listened to the voices of those nearby. Someone said there were maybe five thousand men there plus women and children too. So many people, all eager to hear this Jesus of Nazareth for themselves.

It was a wonderful day and Jesus kept talking and talking and many people were healed too.

I couldn't believe what I was hearing. His stories were so easy to listen to and he made us laugh often. It was all so fresh and new and I could have listened to him for ever. I was so interested, I even forgot to eat!

The end of the day soon came though and we were far from home and it was getting late.

His followers talked together for a while and then they went to talk to Jesus. I began to make my way to the front to see what was happening. They looked concerned and pointed to the direction we had arrived. Jesus shook his head and gestured to them as I watched. One of the group opened his arms and shook his head.

Jesus had finished his teaching and the people were starting to get up so I crept closer.

"Send them away so they can buy themselves something to eat." I caught a little of the conversation.

"You give them something to eat…"

"But we have no food!"

I listened intently. I didn't have much but he could have what I had. It wouldn't go round everyone but at least Jesus could eat.

I stepped forward with my heart in my mouth and offered up my food to one of the men.

"I'm Adam and you can have my food," I said, my voice quivering more than I wanted it to.

The man walked up to Jesus carrying it in his hands.

"We have five small loaves and two small fish here."

"Bring them over here."

Jesus took hold of my food, looked up to heaven and thanked God for the food. Then he broke the loaves into little bits and gave it to his followers, just a little each.

"And don't share it round or you'll be hungry…" Mother's words came back to me.

Mother's not going to be happy, I thought as I glanced back over my shoulder to where my uncle and aunt sat. I watched quizzically as the men begin to share it round amongst the people. It seemed that every time a bit was handed out, there was still some left. They continued to share it out, again and again, until all had eaten and everyone was satisfied.

People even had bread left over and as the disciples went round to collect what was left over, they collected twelve whole basketfuls of food!

I couldn't believe my eyes. And I couldn't wait to tell mother!!

Satisfaction

The people were satisfied! The little boy had given his lunch to Jesus and as a result, many witnessed amazing things.

Why does God urge us to fix our eyes on Jesus and on things that are pure and good and holy?

As we do this, **we take our eyes away from those things which would cause us to be unhappy, worried, jealous and fearful.** When we are surrounded by these negative emotions, it is hard to be satisfied and content.

When we focus on him, we stop comparing ourselves or what we have, with others. We become thankful for having him in our lives and for all the blessings he brings us, however small.

We draw closer to the light, and the darkness of negative stuff diminishes as his size and presence increase in our lives. He is enough and he will prove himself enough, again and again as we keep our eyes fixed on him and live in His love.

When we are as hungry as those people and as obedient as the little child then baskets will overflow in your life in so many ways.

Prayer

Father, nothing in the world compares with you.

Thank you as your light increases in my life the darkness of pain, dissatisfaction and frustration cannot stay.

Increase my hunger I pray as I choose to be obedient to your leading.

Amen

Now read Matthew 14:14-21 – *The Feeding of the Five Thousand*

20

A Few Extra Crumbs

By Isabella (reluctant dog owner)

Dog stared at me for a moment and then picked up the scrap and ran.

In our town, dogs roamed round in packs, forever on the lookout for food but this particular dog used to come every day at the same time. I began looking out for him. He didn't have a name; dogs didn't have names so to me he was just *Dog*.

The dogs have a huge appetite and can never get enough. We would often throw scraps to them and my children would watch them eat, also lapping up any water they might find.

They were very unpopular and some hated them. We heard them howling at night and saw them prowling around the city. They lay in the hot sun dreaming away the afternoon. They crowded around us looking for crumbs after our meals.

Dogs which were used for farming, herding or hunting were the fortunate ones, not treated well but at least most were given a little food. We would see them herding and guarding the sheep on the hillside.

I stood and watched as Dog joined the pack again and ran off into the distance. Suddenly, I heard a shriek. Screaming and bad language emitted from the dwelling next door as my neighbour's demonised daughter threw herself on the floor and rolled around for some minutes.

It wasn't the first time; in fact, it had happened many times. The house was constantly in turmoil and Miriam had explained the cause of the noise to me recently.

The people were Canaanites. Their ancestors lived in the Promised Land prior to the arrival of our people. They worshipped idols and were considered our enemies.

I knew Jesus was visiting our area and the following week myself and my husband made our way to where he was teaching and listened. We had heard so much about this man. His teaching made sense and I could tell my husband was secretly interested in what he was saying.

As we stood there, every so often a woman's voice cried out "Lord, Son of David, have mercy!" Jesus continued but the woman didn't stop shouting. I wished she would be quiet as she was interrupting each time.

Jesus continued his life-giving words.

"Lord, Son of David have mercy!"

"Lord, Son of David have mercy!"

Eventually Jesus stopped and turned. I couldn't see the woman but he beckoned to her and she walked forward. She had a child with her. Suddenly I recognised Miriam! The Canaanite woman. I couldn't believe my eyes. What was she doing here?

"Lord, Son of David have mercy!" she called out again. "My daughter is demon possessed and suffering."

Jesus looked at her thoughtfully.

"Send her away. She's shouting out at us all the time," said one of his followers.

"I am here for the lost lambs of Israel," he spoke out, almost to himself.

At that, Miriam knelt down right in front of Jesus.

"Lord, help me."

"I can't take the children's bread and throw it down for the dogs," he said to her kindly.

I held my breath. *He was teaching Jews so how did he know that she was a Canaanite?* I thought. *I suppose her dress? Her accent?*

But Miriam was not to be deterred.

"Even the dogs get the crumbs under the table." She looked up at him with desperation in her eyes.

Jesus continued to look at her thoughtfully.

"Woman," he said at last. "Your faith is great. I will do what you ask." The crowd gasped.

I looked at Miriam's daughter. She had been in turmoil and now she looked different immediately. Her face was relaxed, her posture was straighter and there was light in her eyes. As she walked away smiling. I knew she was healed.

The next morning, I made sure that I threw a few extra crumbs down for Dog when he came. It's only right, isn't it?

Turmoil

Mental turmoil is not comfortable. It invades our days and nights, our social lives and our times of relaxation. At times, most of us, experience it.

Early on in my life, during a period of turmoil, I gradually learned to **turn those worries and fears into prayers.** I allowed myself a time to visit them daily with God. For me it was a way forward out of the turmoil.

We are told in God's word *"Do not worry...."* but if we're honest, sometimes there is a process to reach that place. For me, to have this time each day helped me take control, then gradually give God control and in that way, I moved forward.

Someone once said *I'm an old man and **I've known many troubles, most of which never happened...***

We know that worry and turmoil won't change anything except deplete our strength but it's hard to stop when we have issues to face. My *what if* time with God helped me to **keep my life free from turmoil for many hours of the day** as I asked him for help and strength to go back out to face them once again.

As we take what he gives, he takes our turmoil and gives us the faith to know that he is in control and in time we find that we can leave these things in his care for good.

Prayer

Thank you Lord, that when my world is in turmoil you are my safe place.

You are my place where everything is calm.

As I visit that place and turn my worries into prayers, you hear me.

Thank you that you are in control.

Amen

Now read Matthew 15:21-28 – ***The Canaanite's Daughter***

21

Far and Wide

By Philip (disciple)

"Philip? Why are we going this way?" I glanced at Nathanial as he walked by my side.

I couldn't understand why we were going this way either. We had travelled north from Tyre and then right through Sidon. I wondered if Jesus planned to get some peace and quiet as it had been such a busy time. Sometimes, recently, we hadn't even had time to eat! We were telling people not to say where we were but it seemed impossible to keep Jesus' presence a secret for long.

We eventually arrived in the area of Decapolis, a group of ten cities with some smaller settlements. Decapolis, a largely Gentile region, had some important trade routes through it and after the isolation of where we had just been, these cities seemed packed with people.

We made our way through the city, trying our best to stick together and keep an eye on Jesus at the front of our group. After a while we reached an area with less people and stopped for a rest. A group of men walked up to us, pointing to one in their midst.

"What do you want?" James asked the man.

The man produced grunting noises and pointed to his ears that he could not hear. He couldn't seem to speak either. I was tired and I closed my eyes in the hot sun. But Jesus looked up at the man, listening intently to the sounds coming from his lips. It was like the man was saying something important, such was Jesus' attention.

His friends begged Jesus to lay his hand on him but instead, Jesus took hold of the man and led him away out of the crowd.

I looked across, interested.

Jesus stood in front of the man and put his fingers in his ears, standing still for a moment.

Then he spat into his hand and reached out and touched the man's tongue with his spittle.

He looked up to heaven and sighed a long deep sigh, as though he felt real compassion for the man and for the horrible way he had to live. Then he said in a loud voice,

"Be opened."

The man looked at Jesus for a moment and Jesus spoke to him. As I watched, the man clearly answered. I could see his lips moving. He could hear and he could reply.

By that time, there were people drawing closer and they were overwhelmed with what was taking place.

Jesus looked around.

"Don't tell anyone what you have seen," he said to the people.

But the people were excited and they rushed off, talking about it even as they went. I just knew they would spread it far and wide.

Loneliness

How many people, although they can listen and speak, feel like they can't? Isolation and loneliness affect many people today.

Loneliness doesn't depend on how many friends you have or how many people are around you. It depends on how emotionally or socially connected you feel. **Loneliness is not being alone. It is a perception of seeing ourselves as alone.** It has less to do with our circumstances and more to do with how we feel about those circumstances.

Loneliness is said to have a detrimental effect on our physical wellbeing. We feel that we are separated and therefore, we are 'less than'. This creates an expectation that we will be alone and it creates a self-fulfilling prophecy.

If you are lonely there are things you can do: contact any friends you do have, always assume you will be the one to instigate things, plan things to look forward to, volunteer to help, attend or get involved in a church, get a pet, spend more time outside, become a giving person and most of all make Jesus your very best friend. He will never let you down, will always be there, has everything you need and is only a prayer away.

As you read these words let him lead you out of that place and let him touch you afresh. **Go out and try to be 'God with skin on' to one person every day** and you will find he has set you free.

Prayer

Thank you Lord, that you are the best friend I will ever have.

But Father, would you raise up other people in my life?

Would you make me a parent to someone and a child to another?

Would you make me a friend to one, a sibling to another and a mentor to others?

Amen

Now read Mark 7:31-37 – ***The Deaf and Dumb Man***

22

Up the Mountain

By Shira (servant)

I packed the bread into the bag, followed by dried olives and figs, smoked fish and some dates. I had also made barley bread the day before and I knew the food would easily last a couple of days.

I was excited, as usually my master and wife travelled alone with little Samson but this time I was to go with them in search of Jesus, this man we had heard so much about.

It wasn't too far but it was hot and the road was dusty and with Samson, our progress was slow.

"Take Samson for a while Shira, would you?" my master's wife had said as she placed him in my arms.

We eventually arrived and followed masses of people to the field where Jesus would be. This was the biggest crowd I had ever seen. There were thousands of people – men, women and children all waiting to hear what this man had to say. It was noisy; men coming and going, women talking and children crying.

Jesus appeared a little way up the mountain in front of us, then he stood and began to speak and it all went quiet apart from the bleating of the sheep in the distance.

The hills around us and the water nearby became a perfect amphitheatre for amplifying his voice so we could clearly hear him. But immediately he stressed that hearing was not enough and we were to listen with our heart as well as our ears.

The day flew past as he told us things we'd never heard before. We slept that night where we sat and the next day, we again were confronted with things we'd never considered before.

We were sitting quite near to the front and I loved watching the group with Jesus interact with each other as they laughed and chatted together.

We saw miracles, real miracles, as the dumb began to speak and blind men began to see. There were many, many sick who were healed. We couldn't always hear but we could see by the way they danced round and glorified God.

By the time the third day came, sadly, we knew that we would have to leave as all our food was eaten up. We were beginning to gather our things together, as were others, when Jesus stood and commanded the people to sit down again on the ground.

He closed his eyes and began to pray for some loaves of bread and what appeared to be some fish which were placed on a huge rock beside him.

He thanked God for the food we were about to eat but on opening my eyes, I could see only seven loaves and a few fish. Hardly enough for thousands of people.

Nevertheless, the men with him crowded round as they received either a fish or a loaf and then began to make their way towards the different groups of listeners sitting on the ground. They just kept giving and the people just kept eating.

Eventually, after several hours, everyone was full and the same men gathered up and passed along to the front all that was left over.

As I watched, the men filled seven basketfuls with the spare food!

People were amazed as they packed up their things and began the journey home.

"How many people do you think were there?" My master's wife asked him.

"I guess about four thousand men plus women and children," he replied.

She turned to me.

"I wish you could do that with our food, Shira" she said, as we made our weary way back home.

Generosity

Generosity is vital to a happy and healthy life.

What we feel thankful for is very important to the quality of our life. When we cause others to be thankful, that is even more important.

For many years generosity has been considered a selfless act. It now appears that there is just as much benefit to the person being generous as to the receiver.

When we are generous, it has some amazing benefits. It enhances our sense of purpose, reduces our stress and gives health to our immune system.

God loves us to be generous and he continually encourages us to do that. To share kind words, generous actions, help others, move in our giftings, display the fruits of them and love our neighbour as ourselves. He knows that as we shift our eyes off ourselves and look to the needs of others, it not only benefits them but it quiets our negative feelings and brings us a sense of worth in giving to someone else. It connects us to one another and we become salt and light in the world just as he planned.

Why not make generosity a fresh life value and look for ways to give to those around you? A chat, a smile, a gift, an email, a phone call, a text, a prophecy, a card, a letter, an encouragement, a visit, a meal?

It benefits others, it benefits yourself and best of all, it pleases God.

Prayer

Please show me what I can give this day, Lord.

You spent your life giving to other people and I want to do the same.

Increase my gift of giving I pray, that however large or small it may be, others may see you living in me.

Amen

Now read Matthew 15:29-39 – *Feeding the Four Thousand*

23

Tree Spotting

By Levi (father of Joshua)

I'd always loved trees, ever since I was small. I loved the tall ones which seem to reach to the sky and have roots deep underground. I used to imagine where the roots stretched to. I loved the ones which bore fruit and would stand radiant in their blossom before the fruit appeared.

Joshua, my son, was the same and I often taught him about the different trees we would pass on a journey and those which grew nearby.

Cedars, I told him, were the symbol of majesty, fertility and abundance. Sycamore trees grew tall and strong and seemed to reach to the sky. Acacia trees were used for wood and charcoal and the cypress tree used for musical instruments.

Joshua would sit and hear how walnut trees were the favourite of many rulers, fig trees provided their delicious fruit and olive trees produced olive oil and ripe olives which we so enjoyed every day.

The list was endless and on every walk, my son's mind would be filled with so many interesting questions and facts.

That was until it all changed.

My left eye was the first to deteriorate and once it began, it rapidly left me with little sight. And then my right quickly followed. Doctor after doctor failed to find a cure until we had spent more than we could afford.

And so, my long walks with Joshua stopped and although we still walked a little, the roles were reversed and it was he who described to me the trees we would pass along the way and tell me their names and their uses.

For many months I felt useless and trapped in my world of darkness.

One day, Joshua came to me and told me I was going into Bethsaida with some friends, to find the man called Jesus who made blind men see.

I'd heard about this Jesus before. Some men from our village, Peter, Andrew and Philip had gone to join Jesus' group and I'd heard about the miracles which had been happening when the thousands of people were fed nearby.

Soon, I too had arrived at where I understood this Jesus was to be.

By the end of the day, a long day when I had listened to the sights and sounds, the oohs and aahs, the laughter and celebrations of people being healed, I was getting tired and going to suggest that we left. I stood little chance with all this crowd of ever getting near Jesus let alone getting healed.

At that moment someone grabbed my hand, pulled me to my feet and led me forward to Jesus begging him to touch me. I felt strong hands take my arm and lead me forward. We kept walking. I couldn't see, I had no idea where we were going. We walked and walked. I could hear the hubbub of the crowd growing softer, the children laughing and the babies crying. And still we walked.

Eventually the sound of the people grew distant and I realised we had left the village behind. As you might imagine, I began to panic. *Where am I? Who am I with? How will I get back?* I slowed my step but the man I was with kept walking leading me after him.

And then we stopped. I heard this man spit on his hands then he placed them on my eyes. We waited for a moment.

"Do you see anything Levi?" a kind voice asked me.

I opened my blind eyes and tried to look around. There was a slight change. I looked around some more. I could see what looked like a few small trees walking around. No faces or hands or feet, just blurred shapes.

Jesus put his hands on my eyes once again and held them there. My eyes were getting hot. There was definitely something happening!

After a moment, he stood back and I looked around. I gasped as I saw people who were leaving the village, real people with arms and legs and bodies. I blinked several times. Was this a dream? I could see as clearly as when I was a child.

"Go straight home from here," Jesus instructed.

"Don't even go back into the village. Go home."

"I knew he would do it," said Joshua as we ate our bread and olives the next day.

Joshua and I were going on a trip. Tree spotting! Who knows, we might even make the Cedars of Lebanon!!!

Vision

This man's life was transformed because he came into the presence of Jesus.

No longer can we stand beside Jesus of Nazareth in his earthly form but we can enter his presence through the Holy Spirit whenever we choose.

We have read how things changed for this blind man. Not immediately, but little by little he began to see.

Vision is a good thing.

But as Christians we don't simply want our own vision but we need to check in to God's vision for our life. **When we get on the right pathway, then things happen for us.** Doors open and blockages dissolve. All we do is walk, step by step closely watching where he leads.

Sometimes it's hard to see the way ahead. We are like that man who couldn't see. Sometimes we see a little but our sight is blurred and we view things *as trees walking*. Sometimes it's crystal clear as we step ahead confidently, knowing that we are in the centre of God's plan.

One thing's for sure, **the way we get vision is by spending time in God's presence.** Little by little things become clear as we keep walking, allowing the peace of God to guide and direct our actions.

Prayer

Father, please help me to walk by faith, not by sight.

Help me to follow your pathway step by step, knowing what you have for me is good, as little-by-little, things become clear.

Give me eyes to see what you write and let that vision grow in me.

Thank you for your perfect plan for my life.

Amen

Now read Mark 8:22-26 – ***The Blind Man***

24

A Smile on His Face

By Gad (father of Hosea)

I summoned up every ounce of courage I had and walked up to the group of men.

"Excuse me, my name is Gad." I heard myself saying. "Please…will you heal my son?"

Hosea stood by my side. I longed for him to live a normal life like his siblings. He tried so hard.

I would often watch my children play together. They loved to play games. Marbles or leap frog or imagination games of weddings or funerals.

We lived, as many did, in an extended family with my parents, grandparents and us and our children, two aunts, one uncle, cousins and in time grandchildren I expect.

Children are a blessing and gift from God and those who live to the age of my boy are precious. Losses are common and it's a fact that often a woman needs six pregnancies to gain two or three living children.

I praised God that my son was alive, but many times his life had been in danger. He would be playing with his siblings and then suddenly a great seizure would take over his body and he would fall and shake and foam at the mouth.

Several times he had fallen into the fire and only the other week, we were walking by a pool and he overbalanced into the water as yet another seizure began without warning. We were at our wits end and I worried so much for his future.

"Gad, leave him to God," I told myself often but still I worried.

The men who were followers of this Jesus had prayed for him and sent us on our way but nothing changed, the seizures just kept coming.

I don't know what made me go back to them but the next time we went, Jesus was with them. Immediately I ran up to Jesus and knelt before him.

"Lord, have mercy on my son." Hosea stood back with his mother.

"He has seizures. He often falls into the fire or the water, please help us Lord," I heard myself saying.

I explained to Jesus how I had already brought him once and the men had prayed but nothing had happened. He was not healed.

Jesus turned and said something to them. He turned back.

"Bring the boy here to me."

He looked down at him with eyes of compassion as my son stared up into his face. Then he spoke, his words seeming to pierce the atmosphere.

"Demon, come OUT," he commanded with an authority I had never heard before.

My son cried out and he clattered to the ground and started to writhe about on the floor. But it did not continue as it usually did.

I looked down at him, my heart beating fast.

For a moment he lay there still and then slowly he began to move and I bent down to help him to his feet.

He looked different. He had a light in his eyes and a smile on his face.

"Father, I am healed," he said quietly as he put his hands out and looked around at the people as though seeing them all for the first time.

I turned for a moment as we walked away. Jesus was in conversation with his disciples. No doubt he had lots to say to them.

Worry

This father must have been incredibly worried about his son.

Falling into water, falling in the fire, his parents must have been never off their guard, worry controlling their thoughts day and night.

The war for our own thoughts is raging also and sometimes we are not even aware of it. Once we understand that fact, we can start to change it.

Our thoughts affect our emotions so **we have to be careful to choose our thoughts** and if a negative thought comes to us, it doesn't mean we have to nurture it. If we feed the negative thoughts in our mind, they drain us of energy and strength.

It's often not our circumstances that make us unhappy but our thoughts about our circumstances.

God hasn't promised us a trouble-free life but he has promised us that when we are being renewed in the spirit of our mind, and we fix our thoughts on what is true and pure and holy, that he will give us peace and strength and courage.

The bible states that as a man thinks in his heart, so he will become. He has plans for you to achieve great things on this earth and that starts in your mind.

Prayer

Help me Lord, to fix my mind on what is true and noble and pure and holy.

Help me to guard my mind and to be more aware of the battleground it can become.

When negative thoughts fill my mind, help me, Lord, to make a choice to fix my mind on what is healthy and wholesome.

Amen

Now read Matthew 17:14-18 – ***The Demoniac Son***

25

The Light is Here

By Dorcas (mother of Samuel)

The birth was not a difficult one. I had been accompanied by a midwife who guided me through and I was so excited to have my first baby.

After birth he was washed, rubbed with salt and wrapped in swaddling clothes, as usual. We immediately gave him a name and we loved Samuel from the start.

It was as he grew that we noticed he didn't see things as other babies did and very soon it was obvious that little Samuel was blind. My disappointment was indescribable.

As he got older, he couldn't play properly with other children and our hearts broke for him. As he grew out of childhood, blindness meant he couldn't work and so as not to be a burden on our family he would go and beg in the streets and bring home the little he had collected. I couldn't face seeing my son there begging at the side of the road and avoided walking that road home.

And now, here I was this Sabbath day, with Samuel standing before this man called Jesus.

"Rabbi, who sinned, he or his parents?" I heard one of his followers ask, as they stood around him.

I had long wondered that question myself. *Why do these things happen? Why had my boy been the one to suffer all these years?*

Jesus turned to him and said, "No one sinned my friend, neither this man nor his parents. This happened so that God may work in him and be seen by men. We must do God's work when the light is here."

He stopped for a moment as if he were thinking.

"I…am the light of the world."

Everyone looked at him, some puzzled, some nodding in agreement and some in the crowd shaking their head.

He looked around at them and then spat on the ground.

He mixed the spittle in the mud with his sandal and then bent and picked some up. Everyone watched as he smeared it across Samuel's eyes.

I watched intently as my son stood trustingly allowing him to do this.

"Go!" said Jesus.

I thought he was sending us home, but he continued.

"Go now and wash in the pool of Siloam."

The pool of Siloam was a safe water supply nearby, and a major gathering place for Jews who were making pilgrimages to the city. I knew it well.

We made our way there and I watched in wonder as my son bent to wash his eyes, blinking as the sunlight bathed his eyelids as for the first time in his life, he began to see.

I couldn't believe that he could actually see and I just marvelled as we made our way back to where Jesus had been.

"Isn't this the blind man who used to sit and beg?" shouted a woman in the crowd as she caught sight of him.

"Yes, I am that man," replied my Samuel, directly to her.

"How did that happen?" shouted someone else.

"The man called Jesus of Nazareth made some mud and put it on my eyes. He told me to go and wash my eyes in the pool of Siloam so I went and did that and then I could see," repeated my son.

A week later we were in front of the Pharisees attempting to explain how my son had been blind all his life and now he could see.

The Pharisees were divided once they heard the story. Some said Jesus of Nazareth was not from God but they were puzzled at how he could do this thing.

"Is this man your son and was he blind?" they asked Samuel and myself."

We replied in the affirmative.

"But how can he see?" they asked.

"Ask him yourself," my husband replied. We did not want to risk being sent out of the synagogue by giving our opinion.

They asked Samuel and he described the miracle.

"But what did he do, how did he do it?"

"Why do you ask me again? Do you want to become his disciples?" my son replied. I held my breath.

They began to get annoyed and after more talk they threw him out of the building.

We were on our way home when suddenly Jesus appeared walking towards us. He had heard of our experience.

"Do you believe in the Son of Man?" he said to my son. "He is speaking to you now."

There was something in the air that you couldn't deny and we worshipped him there and then.

"Lord, I believe," said Samuel as he looked around at all the new things there were to see.

Disappointment

How disappointed must this woman have been to find out her baby was born blind?

Disappointment is the emotion we experience when our hopes or expectations are unfulfilled. It is an inevitable part of living.

There is a mountain in Australia called Mount Disappointment. The view was disappointing to the explorers who climbed it, hence it's unusual name.

Sometimes in life we metaphorically climb this mountain. It's a long slog up as **we have to give ourselves time to acknowledge and accept our situation as it is, not as we hoped it would be.** We fix our eyes on the path ahead and start to climb putting our thoughts in perspective with the life we live.

It's no good looking back at what might have been or looking at others, it doesn't help. If that's you, don't beat yourself up that you hurt, just allow God to pour on his healing as you slowly climb. Keep climbing and **simply allow yourself to look at other views and scenes as they unfold.**

Some disappointments are dealt with in a day and others take many years to deal with. But come the day, come the hour we reach the top of this mount and see a new vision of all that is before us.

Prayer

There are times, Lord, that I have been disappointed.

I have felt that my hopes have been unfulfilled and it's hurt.

Help me to handle disappointment well: to take time to accept my situation, to put my thoughts in perspective and allow you to heal me and watch as new scenes unfold before me.

Amen

Now read John 9:1-38 – *Blind from Birth*

26

The Crowd Cheered
By Areli (good friend)

We had risen early that day to get to the synagogue where we regularly went to worship each Sabbath.

We women walked behind our husbands and on entering the building, I settled down with my mother and daughter while my husband took his place in the men's area.

Levana was not far away from us. She wasn't actually able to see what went on but she was always there and that didn't stop her from being part of the crowd of people who came to worship each week.

She stared down at my feet. I knew that she didn't know who I was.

She turned her head and attempted to see out of the corner of her eye by looking up and sideways.

"Is that Areli?" she said.

I bent down, smiling as she greeted me.

That's how she looked at the world nowadays and her bent back worsened by the year. Physicians were common and numerous but she had been like this for eighteen long years. Her back was set and no matter how hard she tried to stand straight, it was impossible.

Preparing meals, she told me, had become very difficult and any physical work such as grinding the grain was impossible. Baking the bread, making clothes and washing them was very difficult and carrying a jar of water, she had not done that for a long, long time. I knew that she missed meeting and keeping up with the news from the other women at the well.

On this particular day there was an excited buzz as people filed into the synagogue. There was to be a visiting prophet and preacher from Galilee; Jesus of Nazareth would be preaching in our synagogue.

As Jesus begun to preach, the room went silent, all eyes on this man. The time flew.

Eventually he finished his preaching and looked around the room. Suddenly, his gaze rested on Levana and he reached out and beckoned to people near her to bring her forward.

We waited while she slowly and painfully made her way to the front, her eyes never leaving the floor. She couldn't even look up into his face but gazed down at his feet as she stood before him. He looked down at her deformed body.

"Daughter of Abraham, you are set free from your sickness!" He spoke out in a loud, commanding voice.

Some people gasped and the whole room stayed silent to see what would happen.

Then he reached out and laid his hands on her. As they stood together, it was imperceptible to begin with but slowly she began to move, and as the crowd stared at what was taking place hardly daring to believe, she began to straighten her back.

"Look at that, Levana!" My mother's voice was filled with wonder.

Within a minute or so, Levana was standing looking up into the face of Jesus of Nazareth.

The crowd around her went wild. They were cheering and praising God.

And then the synagogue leader held up his arms and the people grew silent as they looked at the faces of the leaders.

"There are six days for work," a voice rang out accusingly.

Jesus turned to the leader.

"Do you not give water to your donkey or ox on the Sabbath?" he asked them. "Then should not this woman who has been sick for eighteen years be set free on the Sabbath?"

The men looked humiliated and the crowd around them once again cheered.

Freedom

"Daughter of Abraham, you are free from your sickness!"

I wonder if this woman ever believed she would hear those words spoken over her life?

Freedom is what everyone desires. No one wants to be in bondage to anything which affects their life in a negative way.

And yet freedom is an anomaly! Our society today has departed from many rules which have been guidelines for humanity for thousands of years.

'Do what you want, when you want, how you want, with whom you want.' 'If it feels right for you, do it.' 'You have a right to do what you want with your own life and your own body as long as it hurts no one else.'

For many people today, following a set of rules or guidelines is considered old fashioned and obsolete.

And yet we see the results of living as we please; men and women bound by financial, physical, emotional and mental chains.

It is when we follow healthy guidelines set up for our good that we find the way to live a life of abundance, free from the chains that life would seek to place on us.

Pursuing freedom is quite the opposite of what you would expect. *"It is for freedom that Christ has set us free"* and it's hard to understand how it works but it does!

Prayer

Thank you Lord, for the guidelines which are written in your word.

Guidelines which bring me freedom and help me find the way to live a life of abundance.

You set me free to live in freedom, Lord.

Thank you that you provide a way for me to live free from those things that would drag me down.

Amen

Now read Luke 13:10-17 – ***The Bent Woman***

27

We Watched the Man Walk Away
By Cyrus (a prominent Pharisee)

Monday and Thursday were our days of fasting and on the other days we ate. It was Tuesday and we had a visitor.

I always did my very best to follow not only the fasting rules, but all the rules and I had competently completed my year of probation as a Pharisee.

I was proud of my achievement. Paying my tithes and reciting my prayers in the morning and the evening, I loved the public prayer at street corners and the entrance to the synagogue, demonstrating my adherence to God.

When I fasted, I put ashes on my head and wore old clothing to demonstrate my commitment to God.

Learning the elaborate system of hand washing, running the water to my wrist and then running the water down my hands, off my fingers; after a while it became a natural habit which I didn't even need to think of.

I sincerely wanted to avoid eternal punishment and receive eternal life so it was important that I learned to follow those rules.

I progressed up the ranks and soon I was known as a 'prominent pharisee'. Not only keeping the rules myself, I ensured the people did the same, and also took a position of authority among other pharisees which was more than I had hoped for.

This particular day, I had a visitor. Jesus of Nazareth was coming to my house! This man was an anomaly. He appeared to do so much good but he caused so much trouble and went out of his way to cut across all that I considered honourable.

He attracted huge multitudes of people, crowds everywhere. He was very popular with the common man. Instead of telling the people what to do, it seemed that he delighted in breaking the very rules we were training them to follow! One day, he even had dinner with a tax collector!

He seemed to have no regard for their sin and he destroyed the moral standards we had set for the people. He hated the deeds of people like myself. He said that we were painted on the surface but inside were filled with dead men's bones. Clean on the outside but filthy inside. This man intrigued me though.

But I did fear an uprising, that we would lose our authority and power and it would bring a bloodbath, and so I knew that there would be others at my house carefully watching this Jesus as he visited.

"Greetings Cyrus." Our guests acknowledged me as they entered but I knew they only had eyes for one man that day.

Jesus arrived and the room started to fill up with the most prominent pharisees and some lawyers also. I had ensured that some ordinary people had been invited into the courtyard so that they could meet Jesus of Nazareth too.

We sat round the table, the meal was served and we began to speak together.

We talked for a long while and Jesus had much to say and then he turned to those common people who were trying to listen in the courtyard. There was a man at the front. His body was swollen and he was obviously suffering.

Then Jesus turned back to us.

"Is it lawful to heal on the Sabbath or not?" he asked.

The room was silent.

He stood up and walked across to the man and laid his hands on him. Everyone at the table was watching closely.

The room was still as the swelling all over his body started to reduce. We sat in silence until all the swelling was gone and the man was a normal size.

"I tell you…" Jesus continued, "if you had an animal that fell into a pit on the Sabbath, wouldn't you pull it out?"

No one said a word as we watched the man walk away totally healed.

Hospitality

The earliest signs of hospitality are said to be thousands of years ago. In ancient cultures, strangers were welcomed and offered food, shelter and safety. Certainly, in bible times hospitality was very important and we see that even this prominent Pharisee was welcoming people to his house.

We are encouraged to be hospitable in our own lives today. **Hospitality is creating space for others to be themselves. You are providing them with comfort and giving them the message that you trust them and they can trust you. You are sending the message that it's OK to be who they are** and that you accept them without judgement.

Hospitality feeds a most basic need to feel loved and accepted and as we practise this, it deepens our relationships.

In striving to meet the needs of others we are satisfying our own need also. It has many benefits to us.

It is human nature to connect with others. As we open our life and our home to others, the effect lasts! Relationships deepen and develop and change as a result of time spent together.

In fact, we could find that we get more out of our hospitality gift than others do. Whatever happens, God will bless you as you reach out.

Prayer

Would you lead me, Lord, to those with whom you want me to share what I have?

Father, let my life flow with hospitality to those you lead me to.

Show me simple things that people feel they can return and out of these, may there grow friendships that last.

Amen

Now read Luke 14:1-6 – *The Man With Dropsy*

28

Is There Only You?
By Zebedee (very thankful former Leper)

Nathan, Rafael, Tzion, Uri, Itamar, Yuval, Ephraim, Nissan and Medad stood quietly in a line by my side. Me? I am Zebedee.

They were Jewish, I was a Samaritan but we had one thing in common. And that one thing seemed to override the fact that I was considered a loathed, despised, half-breed. The kind of person that most Jews would think unclean.

It was a year before that day that the itching started, I remember it well as it was the day after the Sabbath rest. After that, my skin began flaking and developing sores.

I knew the rules for leprosy, and I tore my clothes and let my hair remain unkempt and with an incredibly heavy heart, moved outside the town! It broke my heart to leave my wife and three children and new baby daughter and I cried as I went.

I had lost my life as I knew it.

I wandered around homeless, begging what I could and shouting 'unclean, unclean,' whenever I came near to people.

I don't know why I shouted. With my torn clothes and obvious skin sores, it was evident I was a leper. I certainly didn't need a doctor to tell me. Very occasionally leprosy would go away by itself but for most, there was no known cure.

Worst of all was the fact that everyone could see my condition and no doubt had their own ideas of what I'd done to deserve what I'd got. It didn't matter so much with strangers, but my reputation was ruined before those I worked with and my neighbours and friends.

My discomfort and pain were my own fault. Everyone knew it and no one came to help for fear of sinning themselves.

Because I was a Samaritan, I had little company but when I heard that my fellow lepers were planning this journey, my heart leapt and I was determined to go with them.

Jesus and his followers were travelling right along the border between Galilee and Samaria and we could not miss this chance to see him. We had heard that he was travelling to Jerusalem and would be coming through a nearby village so we waited in hope.

We stood in line, the other nine lepers and myself and we called out to him from a distance.

Ephraim shouted across.

"Jesus, Master, have pity on us!"

Jesus stopped and looked over at us one by one and then he shouted back.

"Go and show yourselves to the priests." He continued to walk on. Then he was gone.

We stood looking at each other, our white flaky skin was still very evident but there was something in his words which gave me a seed of hope, a flicker of faith deep down.

Some of the group looked disappointed.

"Well let's at least do what he says," I said.

"But we can't go to the priest looking like this, Zebedee." Uri sat down in the dust.

In the end we agreed to go and find the priests.

We tried to avoid people as we went to find the local synagogue. The young men of the village were in the school there, busy studying the Scriptures.

We stood outside and one of the priests came out to see what we wanted. We stood at a distance but all the time the seed was growing within me.

"What do you want?" he asked us.

I turned to my brothers ready to explain that Jesus of Nazareth had sent us to see them and as I did, I stopped still, for their skin was perfectly healthy once again.

"I… I… er… Jesus sent us to show you … our … er … healing …" I stuttered, amazed at what I saw before me.

The priest looked at us for a moment and then walked back inside and my brothers went wild. They danced and jumped and shouted and then ran off to show their families that they were healed.

I stood there alone. I longed to share the good news but there was something I had to do first.

I made my way back to where Jesus was. It took me a while to find him, but when I reached him, I threw myself at his feet. My heart was overflowing with gratitude.

"Thank you, thank you, thank you…" I said over and over again.

"Is there only you who has come back to say thank you?" he asked me, looking round.

I remained silent as I didn't know what to reply.

"Get up and go," he replied. "Your faith has made you well."

I stood and looked at my hands back and front. Hands that could now work and labour and love. I had plans.

The very first thing I would do is to pick up my baby daughter and that would be just the start….

Gratitude

Gratitude is one of the most well researched concepts in psychology today and there are many benefits to having a thankful attitude in life, whatever your circumstances.

The psychologists say that gratitude has many benefits. It can improve your sleep; help you achieve your goals and give you positive emotions. It helps you really enjoy your good experiences, it improves your health, helps you deal with problems and enhances your relationships. It certainly does make you happier.

The great thing about being thankful is that you don't need an awful lot of possessions to practise it. We can be thankful for waking up today, our health, our friends, our home and our family. And we don't even need to have all of these things. **We learn to focus on what we have, not on what we haven't!**

The bible urges us to be thankful and to make gratitude a part of every day. As our gratitude grows, so too will our sense of joy and peace and happiness.

Prayer

Lord, I am grateful for so many things.

Thank you for my friends and family and my church and the finance you provide.

Please open my eyes to those things I don't see, that I can truly live a grateful life every day.

Amen

Now read Luke 17:11-19 – ***The Ten Lepers***

29

If Only You'd Been Here
By Mary (awestruck sister)

I looked around the room. The room was full but I felt alone. My sister had set off a while ago and the only ones left were the mourners who had come to comfort us in our grief.

"It's too late," we said to each other. "If he had only been here our brother would be alive."

We lived in Bethany only two miles from the city of Jerusalem. Bethany was on the hillside, one of the villages scattered throughout the countryside. We worked the land, tended the flocks, worked our trade and we rarely left the confines of our village.

We had a little one storey house made of stone. The houses surrounded a town square where there were some shops, a market and a communal well.

We had a carpenter, a blacksmith, a shoemaker, a potter and a weaver so we could get all we needed there. Many of the men worked in the fields and most families kept a few sheep or goats. From them, we got milk and wool and leather and food. Shepherds tended flocks on the hillside.

In the evening some of the men gathered in the synagogue for a service and scripture discussion.

We went to Jerusalem occasionally and always once a year to celebrate the Passover.

Jerusalem had walls and gates and a watchtower where the watchmen could protect the city. The city was a very busy place, the streets were narrow and the homes came right up to the edge of the street.

Upon entering through the huge city gates into the marketplace there was much noise and activity everywhere. The city gates were where business took place, legal matters were decided, social gatherings happened, children played and religious leaders congregated. It was very different to Bethany.

My mind snapped back to the present.

My sister had arrived back. "Mary… the teacher is here," she said to me urgently, "and he is asking for you."

"What happened?" I asked anxiously, as she came past the mourners, towards me.

"I found him and told him what happened to Lazarus. I said that if he had been with us when we asked him to come, that he wouldn't have died but could he still help us?"

"What did he say?"

"He said that Lazarus would rise again, but I knew that. He will rise on the last day we know…"

She paused to wipe her brow with her hand.

"He said *'I am the resurrection and the life'* and asked me if I believed that. I said of course I do and then he said 'go now and fetch Mary'."

Jesus was standing outside the village when we reached him.

He looked at the two of us and the distraught people who had followed us.

"Where have you laid him?" he simply asked us and as he followed us he looked deeply moved as he looked at the two of us. His eyes were awash. Tears rolled down his face into his beard.

We stood together at the entrance to the tomb. He said little.

"Remove the stone," he requested, and the large covering to the tomb was removed.

"He's been dead for four days," Martha reminded him. "There will be a terrible smell in there."

But Jesus didn't go in. He simply commanded in a loud voice,

"LAZARUS… COME OUT…"

As we watched nothing happened for a moment then there was movement inside the tomb and slowly our brother, wrapped in grave clothes, came and stood before us!

I felt disbelief and joy and anxiety and awe all at once. I didn't know what to feel but I knew, as we removed the grave clothes around him that our brother had been dead for four whole days and he now stood right in front of us, alive and well and ready for a whole new adventure in life.

Many of the mourners were filled with awe and wonder. There were just some who turned and left. I knew they had Pharisee friends and I knew exactly where they were headed!

Empathy

Jesus not only demonstrated great empathy for his friends, he felt it too!

Empathy is more than sympathy. Sympathy is a feeling of sorrow for someone's misfortune while empathy is feeling sorrow but also **taking on someone else's perspective.** The capacity for empathy varies from person to person, in other words some people have stronger *mirror neurons* than others.

It's the mirror neurons that make you yawn when someone else yawns, laugh when they laugh and cry when you see someone emotional. It's the mirror neurons that help us empathise with the pain of other people. The more you have the more you are able to identify with others.

Empathy can be inherited to a certain extent. If your mother was very compassionate then you may be so too. It is also encouraged by your environment as you grow up. Living in a caring and compassionate environment or even living through difficult times can also increase your empathy for others.

Having said that, **wherever you are on the empathy scale, it is something that you can develop.**

As Christians there is something powerful in fellowship. It is God's plan that we share together, gain strength from each other and put our empathy to work as we pray for and help each other.

It's God's plan that the world sees our love for each other and feels our empathy as we reach out to them. By this all men will know that we are his disciples.

Prayer

Show me your heart Lord, and let me know your compassion for the world around me.

Teach me to love the unlovely and also those people I really don't like. Use my empathy for others as a magnet to draw people to you.

Amen

Now read John 11:1-45 – *__The Raising of Lazarus__*

30

In My Heart I Knew

By Bartimaeus (Jericho resident)

We sat in that spot most days. Belshazzar and I. For six hours or so every day, there we baked in the sun.

It was a good place to beg as it's the road into Jericho and more than a few rich and powerful men pass by that way. Homeless men line the roads in and out of Jericho, as it's a good place to meet both rich traders and also those involved in politics too.

Jericho, the city of palms. An oasis city. A city so pleasing with its fresh water and warm climate that the palace of Herod the Great is built here. I've never seen it but I've heard it's a magnificent building and is known far and wide.

I heard the beggars calling to one another, voices worn with pain and desperation.

It's good though to smell the fresh air of the country filling my nostrils and I felt the hot sun on my face as I sat hour after hour, day after day hoping for someone to drop a coin in front of me.

I heard sheep being herded and donkeys being driven past by their owners. I heard voices as men walked past, and I could smell the camels as they passed, snorting and dropping their dung on the roadside.

Occasionally all went quiet and I heard the sheep bleating up in the hills. The road was a major thoroughfare for trading caravans and I sometimes heard military personnel passing by too. Some pilgrims passed multiple times a year on their way to visit Jerusalem.

Most people, who travelled the eighteen miles from Jericho to Jerusalem, would journey in groups for it was a dangerous road. Once out of the city, the barren and parched road descends steeply and the majority of those miles are desert conditions with many hiding places for bandits along the way. It was very easy to escape once again back into the desert.

People were an easy target on this isolated road and anyone attacked would have no food or water or shelter, totally exposed. At certain points further along the road, it became so narrow that a traveller had to literally step over someone who had been attacked.

I didn't need to venture onto this dangerous road but sat just outside the city and listened to all who passed by.

I remember that day so clearly. The sun beat down and it had been difficult to find somewhere in the shade when my friend brought me to my place as he did that day. Belshazzar was there already and today he was right next to me. I knew that this day, scattered along this road, there would be many beggars and invalids begging for money on which they would survive.

We talked of nothing in particular but passed the time of day in silence with an occasional comment to each other.

Suddenly, I could hear a crowd advancing. I could hear the sounds of voices as they came nearer. I listened intently.

I knew the rhythm of the day on this road but this was something different. The crowd came closer and closer until the voices were loud in my ears.

"Jesus…" I heard a voice call from within the crowd…

"It's Jesus of Nazareth coming this way," Belshazzar said to me urgently.

Jesus? Jesus of Nazareth? *Was this the Jesus of Nazareth*, I thought, *passing right by where we sat?*

We waited, and then we began calling out loudly.

"Lord, Son of David, have mercy on us." Again and again we called.

I could see nothing but I could hear them. It seemed the group of people had stopped right where we were. I heard voices shout back.

"Be quiet." They were filled with scorn and hatred. "Go away…get out of here…"

But we knew we must persist at any cost.

And then…

"What do you want me to do for you?" I will never forget that voice.

Immediately Belshazzar called back.

"We want our sight."

The crowd went quiet and for a few moments I wasn't sure what was happening.

And then I felt hands, strong hands.

They were touching my eyes. I sat still as I felt the heat of his hands on my eyelids and then my eyeballs and eye sockets.

There was no mistaking it. I knew something was happening.

I don't remember him reaching out to Belshazzar as I was so aware of something wonderful taking place within me. A sensation of heat and power starting in my eyes but producing a wonderful sense of love throughout my whole body.

I slowly opened my eyes, blinking against the bright light, and I saw the terrain around me. I was still burning from the heat within me.

Hands and faces and feet. The stones and the tall palm trees and the green plants. The path before me and the city of Jericho not far away and the steep, arid road stretching towards Jerusalem.

Belshazzar, still sitting at my side, was also gazing around in awe at everything around him.

We jumped to our feet and joined the group. Why wouldn't I? I followed him for a while before I left him to continue his journey but, in my heart, I knew I followed him forever.

Persistence

The bible speaks a lot about persistence. Be it in doing good, in prayer or in facing adversity, Jesus held persistence as a very high value as he shared his parables.

Persistence is acquired not inherited, it's something that we decide to employ.

When we see a goal and feel that the importance of that goal is greater than the pain of getting there, persistence is easy. When the pain of achieving it is greater than the goal itself, then persistence becomes more difficult.

When we have an intensity of focus, a tenacity and determination, then we are much more likely to achieve our goals. **So often, it's not ability but attitude that gets us to the finishing line** and with God on our side, we cannot fail.

As soon as the two blind men heard that Jesus was nearby, they started to shout *'Lord, have mercy on us!'* Even when the crowd rebuked them and told them to be quiet, they didn't stop, they shouted all the louder. They had persistence! The importance of their goal was so much greater than the pain of getting there as the crowd around shouted them down.

God calls us to walk with persistence as we fix our eyes on the eternal goal, he has prepared for us.

Prayer

It is my prayer, Lord that you allow persistence to grow in me.

Give me a tenacity that will not let go, an ability to hold on against all odds and never let go.

Give me a determination to follow what you want and never give up.

May the importance of your command or calling be so much greater than the pain of getting there.

Amen

Now read Matthew 20:29-34 – *The Two Blind Men*

31

Somewhere to Sit

By Asher (confused fig tree owner)

It was early morning and I sat under the large fig tree sheltering from the increasing heat of the late spring sun. Every day I wandered round these trees and then sat under the thick foliage of this tree on the edge of my land. Its size and its large green leaves always provided much appreciated shade especially in the heat of the day.

Samuel should be here soon I thought to myself. He often came to sit with me under this tree.

I have many fig trees growing wild on my land and the deep roots and large branches take up much ground. That's why I bought this land. Having even one fig tree is a sign of wealth and wellbeing and my land is full of them.

We enjoy a twice-yearly crop of delicious figs from these trees. The first crop, just before summer, we eat fresh and the autumn crop, we dry for winter. By December, my fig trees have shed their leaves and remain bare through the winter months until March when they start to sprout their buds once more.

I glanced again up the track for any sight of Samuel. I could see no one.

I looked at the mature leaves above me. It was incredibly early for these leaves to be at this stage. *It's an early bloomer so it should have early figs* I thought to myself. Seeing the mature leaves, I knew that under them should be ripe fruit somewhere up there.

Once picked, we would dry them in the sun, then press them together and make cakes to eat or give away. I would store some and sell some too at the market.

I sat watching the women return from the well as was their habit before the heat of the day arrived. There were people with their donkeys beginning their journey to Jerusalem and others on their way to the market at Bethany.

I noticed a crowd of men coming from Bethany and I realised, as I watched, that amongst them was Jesus of Nazareth. They were shouting to each other and I could hear laughter as they walked together.

"I'm hungry," I heard someone say as they approached.

Before long they were standing right by my tree and Jesus walked over to where I was sitting.

I stood, out of respect for this man of whom I had heard so much, and stepped to the side as the group watched him from the road.

He reached up and moved the large green leaves to look for the fruit underneath. He moved another leaf then another and as he did so, we realised that on this tree there was no fruit! There was nothing on it but leaves.

He stood back and looked at the tree.

"May you never bear fruit again!" he said with disappointment in his voice.

I watched, as before my eyes, over the space of a few moments this healthy fig tree began to wither. I watched hardly believing my eyes.

His disciples were amazed.

"How did that fig tree wither?" I heard one of them exclaim.

By now it was withered and dead.

"I tell you," he replied. "If you have faith, you cannot only do this, but you can say to this mountain go and throw yourself into the sea, and it will take place." I turned and looked at the mountain upon which Jerusalem was built. Could I do that? I doubted it.

He wandered back to the group of men.

"If you believe, whatever you ask for in prayer you will receive it," I heard him say as they walked on.

I stood looking at the fallen leaves around me.

I had no idea where Samuel had got to but he would have to find somewhere else to find shade tomorrow!

Fruitfulness

What is it that causes some Christians to be more fruitful than others? What is it that causes some plants to be fruitless?

Many things affect how much fruit a plant produces. The climate that the young plant exists in is vitally important. The amount of rainfall improves the quality of fruit and strong winds can be damaging to a plant as it grows. Frost can kill it or severely stop it bearing fruit for a couple of years.

So too, the amount of light will play a major role in the fruitfulness of an orchard and balanced nutrition needs to be provided at just the right time. The roots should have space to grow deep and strong and pruning will cause much more fruit to appear.

The bible says *'by their fruit you will know them'* and our lives are to be a shining witness to the one who is living within us.

So many things affect the abundance of our fruit: the climate that we expose ourselves to, allowing the Holy Spirit to water our lives regularly and surrounding ourselves with the love and protection of others when the strong winds of life blow on us. Staying in the warmth of fellowship, staying under the light of God's presence and feeding on God's word every day will bring the beauty of blossom and the abundance of fruit. Lastly, letting our roots grow deep in good strong soil and realising that **any pruning that God does, is ultimately for our good and that he will work all things together.**

It's his plan for us to share his love in the world through the fruits of the Holy Spirit he has placed in us.

Prayer

I want to be fruitful for you Lord God.

I long for your Holy Spirit to pour down over my life.

I want to surround myself with the love and protection of others when trouble comes.

I want to live in the light of your presence so that your beauty and abundance ever flow from my life.

Amen

Now read Matthew 21:18-22 – *The Fig Tree*

32

It Was All a Mistake

By Malchus (servant of the high priest)

The night was hot and the crowds were wild. The disturbing sound of shouts and screams were all around me as I led the High Priest's Temple guard and the party of Roman soldiers to find this man Jesus of Nazareth.

As servant of High Priest Caiaphas, it was my job to accompany them to make sure that everything went according to orders. I was the ear of the High Priest and whenever anything took place of note, I reported back to him.

The High Priest's job is to supervise the rest of the priests and the temple worship and to make sacrifices for the people's sins once a year on the Day of Atonement. There is much to do in the life of the temple and I am assistant to whatever needs to happen.

But this night was like little I had experienced before.

We fought our way through the crowds. We made our way through a garden until we reached the man they called Jesus of Nazareth. He was surrounded by his disciples, some of them standing, some rousing themselves from sleep and some still sleeping. He was telling them to get up.

We stood and waited for the arranged sign. The garden was filling with people. Suddenly, from amidst the crowd there strode a man. He approached Jesus and went up to him to kiss him.

The man Jesus, looked down at him with sadness in his face.

"Judas, are you betraying me with a kiss?" he asked.

But this was the sign we were waiting for and I didn't wait for any reply. I nodded to the temple guards by my side.

At that everyone started to shout.

"Should we strike with our swords?" shouted one of his followers eager to protect their leader. But before Jesus had time to speak, one of them stepped out and brought down his sword upon me. I ducked to one side and he missed my head but his sword cut off my right ear! I didn't realise for a moment and then suddenly the pain was indescribable and I cried out and clutched the side of my head where the blood flowed freely.

"Malchus!!!" I heard my subordinate shout as he saw the blood.

There was much noise around me as I bent over in pain but I clearly heard a voice.

With authority the words of Jesus of Nazareth rang out and cut through the noise around like a knife.

"No more of this!"

And suddenly all was quiet.

I felt his life-giving hands reach out to me and firmly hold the side of my face. He held on for a moment and I felt the heat of his power flowing right through my body.

I stood up straight as the pain left me and when my hand replaced his, upon my wound, I found an ear, my ear, whole and healthy.

I gazed after him as they led him off, still wiping my blood from his hands. Suddenly I knew it was all a terrible mistake. This plan was all wrong. But it was too late to stop and I had played my part.

Protection

We are told many times that when we belong to God, he will protect us. Time and time again we read this in his word. He has promised us safety whatever the circumstances.

But what about when it seems that God allows things to take place in our lives which we wouldn't choose?

We see in our story how Peter attacked the leader of the temple guards. He genuinely tried to protect Jesus when he saw them come towards him. But he was only seeing part of the picture.

As Jesus responded and healed the servant's ear, he knew that these events needed to happen in order to fulfil the plans of his Father. He knew that Peter was destined to lead the church and at that moment, did not need to be arrested and imprisoned for attacking a temple official. **Jesus saw the whole picture while Peter saw just a part.**

When things don't go the way we would want, and it seems that God doesn't protect us from difficulty, he promises that in the big picture somehow, in some way, all things will work together for good, for them that love him.

Sometimes we see our prayers answered quickly, sometimes it takes many years and **sometimes for reasons known only**

to God, we have to learn to live with the mystery of what seems to be unanswered prayer.

Whatever you may face this day, his protection is around you and it is good to know that you are safe, surrounded by his love.

Prayer

Father, when things don't go my way, it's often painful.

Thank you, Lord, that you see the whole picture.

Thank you that every part which I see, belongs to a whole life that's safe in your hands.

I want to trust you more Lord God.

Amen

Now read Luke 22:45-51 – ***The Servant's Ear***

33

Lost For Words

By Nathaniel (disciple)

I still remember that day when Philip came up to me and said they had found him – Jesus of Nazareth, who Moses and the prophets wrote of.

I remember it so well. I was sitting under a fig tree enjoying the peace of the afternoon. It seemed just an ordinary day. I had no idea that my life would change from that moment on.

I was very doubtful at Philip's words. Nazareth? Could anything good come from Nazareth?

I said that to Philip.

"Nathaniel, come and see," he replied not in the least perturbed about my doubts.

We went together to find this Jesus and as we walked towards him, he was already looking out for us.

He turned and looked me up and down.

"Nathaniel," he said as though he had known me all his life. "Behold, a godly man indeed, in whom is no guile!" he continued.

"How do you know me?" I replied.

"I saw you sitting under the fig tree even before Philip called you," he said.

I was speechless.

"Rabbi, Son of God," I uttered.

"Because I said I saw you Nathaniel, is that why you believe? You will see much greater," he continued. "You will see heaven open and the angels of God ascending and descending upon me."

My mind snapped back to the present. Now Jesus was gone, crucified, dead and buried and I didn't know what to believe.

So much had taken place in so little time. Here we were, myself, Simon Peter and Thomas, James and John and two others, walking along the water's edge of the Sea of Tiberias.

It was late in the day and the sun was going down. The fishing boats were bobbing in the water beside us.

"I'm going out to fish," Simon Peter suddenly announced.

"Ok," said another, "I'll come too".

In the end we all decided to go out. We needed food. Our financial source had dried up since Jesus had left us and we were having to resort to fishing to keep ourselves fed.

So, we all climbed into the boat and started to sail out to sea. Soon it was dark, the net was lowered and we settled down.

We talked of the events of the last couple of weeks. So many emotions, guilt, fear, awe, confusion had filled our hearts during this time and we were still trying to make sense of everything.

The empty tomb? The appearance of Jesus to Mary Magdalene, to Mary, Salome and Joanna and then to Simon Peter? Jesus walking on the road to Emmaus and then the twice he appeared to us in the locked room? There were so many questions, so much to take in.

Our conversation went back to when we first got together and some of the funny things that happened and we laughed. And then we cried as we spoke of how we missed him and of the tremendous longing in our heart to be with him again which we felt would never fade." But there was nothing at all in the net.

We wearily began to make our way back to land knowing that we would have to find breakfast another way.

I remember it now. When we were about a hundred yards from the shore, we saw there was a man standing at the water's edge.

The stranger called out to us.

"Friends, do you not have any fish?"

"No fish," we shouted back.

"Throw your net on the right side of the boat. You'll get some there," he replied, cupping his mouth with his hands as he shouted.

For a moment no one moved. But then Simon Peter got up and began to pull the net up. We joined him and moved it over to the other side.

We waited. Very soon I could see the net getting heavier by the minute and within an amazingly short space of time, the net was full of large healthy fish. We were lost for words.

It was evident that it was far too heavy to haul in.

Suddenly John stood to his feet.

"It's the Lord," he said. "It is... it's the Lord!!!"

In an instant, Simon Peter had grabbed his outer cloth and jumped into the water!

We followed in the boat with hearts beating in excitement and a net full of fish.

As we landed, Jesus was standing to greet us with a fire of burning coals and fish cooking by his side. There was bread there too.

"Bring some of the fish you have just caught," he said.

Simon Peter, strong as an ox, climbed back into the boat and dragged the net ashore. I couldn't believe with so many fish, the net had not torn, but it was strong and we had lost not one fish.

We took them out one by one and laid them on the shore. All night catching nothing and then one hundred and fifty-three fish in the last half an hour!

"Come and have breakfast now," Jesus said.

As he shared out the bread and then the cooked fish, my mind went back to the time he fed the huge group of people with five loaves of bread and two fish.

So many memories to hold in my heart.

I looked around me at Jesus and the other six men around him, and as I did there was something deep down which told me that whatever had gone before, somehow, in some way, it had all only just begun.

Hope

To have hope is to desire an outcome that, to our mind, improves a situation in some way. Hope helps make a difficult situation more bearable. It can improve our life by motivating us to work towards a desire. Hope is a vital part of being a human being.

As Christians, we can direct our hopes in prayer and invite God to intervene in our situation and answer us. **He is our light in the darkness, our climbing frame out of the pit and our leader in the wilderness.**

Hope is vital to our existence, important to our success and it brings us comfort even when all seems lost.

God is our ultimate hope because in his word we read about our future when this life is over. When Jesus ascended into heaven, he went to prepare your place.

We need not fear that this life is the end but know as we read his words that our hope in the eternal life that God has given us will take place one day.

As we leave this life, we find out that it's not the end but that it's only just begun.

Prayer

Thank you Lord, that you are my light in the darkness.

That when I see nothing, you shine your light for my feet to follow the way.

Thank you that you are my ladder out of the pit.

Thank you that you are my leader in the wilderness.

Wherever I am, you are my hope and will always be so.

Amen

Now read John 21:1-14 – ***One Hundred and Fifty-Three Fish***

Prayer

If you have been moved or blessed by these stories of Jesus but have never begun your own relationship with Him, why not do that today by praying the prayer below:

Dear God,

Thank you that you are beginning to open my eyes to your world.

I want to say in this moment, here is my heart – I have made some space for you.

I am sorry for my wrong doing and I ask you to forgive my sin and change me from the inside out.

Let your light flood my life and ignite the kingdom life within me.

I ask you to be the rock that never moves in my life, from this day on.

Amen

Other books by Margaret Peat

The White Elephant

Eleven real life stories about people who dealt with issues such as loss, inferiority, shame and forgiveness. A devotional book to work through your own issues as you read.

The Seagull

Eleven more stories about real people dealing with life topics such as putting God in a box, the power of words, the effect of sowing and reaping. Again, a devotional book for you.

Dear Sally

Presented in the form of letters which Margaret sent to a close friend at a difficult time. This book works through eleven powerful life principles for you to weave into your own life and experience.

Great Thoughts from a Little Dog

If you don't like dogs, don't buy this book! A 31 day devotional for dog lovers based on the benefits of knowing God as Father. Enjoy a dog parable a day!

Across the Brook

Kevin and Margaret share their individual stories as they journeyed along their first 25 years of life. This book shows how anyone, whatever their earthly father relationship, can discover a perfect Father's love.

The Journey

A spiritual journey into the presence of God borne out of messages Margaret has preached and ministered over the years. It is packed with wisdom, insight, dynamic practical advice, honesty and a good dose of humour!

The Well and the Woman

You will never read the story of the Samaritan woman who met Jesus at the well in the same light again. Margaret brings this story to life and brings truth that will challenge, bless and inspire. More importantly it will draw you closer to your Heavenly Father as you learn to draw on the source of that *'Living Water'*

Family at War

Based on personal family research over many years, Margaret tells of her family building a new life in Britain and their battles with such things as disillusionment, poverty, heartbreak, sin and prejudice. It then turns that focus to the spiritual battles we face with the same issues and what the bible says using those words as a launch pad into personal victory, prayer and praise.

Little Thoughts from Great Cats

Written both for Christians and those still on their journey to a personal relationship with God, Margaret again draws inspiration from her love of animals bringing together thoughts, insights and words of wisdom that can be relevant to everyone – cat lover or not.

For orders please contact: KMPeat@aol.com